Ultimate Exam Practice

GCSE
exam
secrets

Steven Croft

English
Literature

CONTENTS

To revise any of these topics more thoroughly, see Letts
Revise GCSE English and English Literature Study Guide.

(see inside back cover for how to order)

THIS BOOK AND YOUR GCSE EXAMS

Introduction

This book is designed to help you get better results.

▶ Look at the grade A and C candidates' answers and see if you could have done better.

▶ Try the exam practice questions and then look at the suggested answers.

▶ Make sure you understand the suggested answers and points you are given.

▶ When you are ready, try the GCSE mock exam papers.

If you perform well on the questions in this book, you should do well in the examination. Remember that success in examinations is about hard work, not luck.

What examiners look for

▶ There are not normally 'right' or 'wrong' answers in English Literature. The examiner will assess your work on the quality of your ideas and your expression.

▶ You should make sure that you have ideas about the texts on which you will answer questions.

▶ Your writing should be clearly structured and organised effectively in sentences and paragraphs.

▶ You should be able to communicate your ideas clearly and effectively.

▶ You should use a wide vocabulary to express your ideas and meaning.

Exam technique

▶ You should spend the first few minutes of the exam reading the questions and choosing the ones on which you can produce the best answers.

▶ Make sure you understand the questions that you are going to answer.

▶ Identify what the question is asking you to do – underlining the key words can help.

▶ Plan your answers – do not write down the first thing that comes into your head. Planning is essential if you are to write effective essays on texts.

▶ Do not plan to have time left over at the end. If you do, use it to check your answers for mistakes or things left out.

DIFFERENT TYPES OF QUESTIONS

Although the questions that you will get on the exam papers at the end of the course will all require essay answers, the questions can take different forms. These are described below.

Analysis of a passage or text extract

Sometimes a question will be set on a particular passage or extract from a text. This will be printed on the exam paper and you will be asked a question or questions on it. Sometimes the question will ask you to focus entirely on the passage or it might ask you to consider the passage and then relate it in some way to the text as a whole. You should:

▶ read and understand what the question asks you to do

▶ read the passage or extract through carefully

▶ plan your answer carefully

▶ structure your ideas in a logical way, writing in sentences and paragraphs

▶ make sure that your answer is focused on what the question asks you.

Aspect of texts such as character or theme

Sometimes a question will be set asking you to consider and discuss or explore some aspect of the text you have studied, such as looking at a particular character or theme. You need to:

▶ read and understand what the question asks you to do

▶ focus your answer on the specific topic you have been given

▶ plan your answer carefully

▶ make sure that you are answering precisely what the question asks you.

Questions with more than one part

Sometimes a question will be set that has more than one part to it. Make sure that you:

▶ read and understand all parts of the question before you start to answer

▶ answer all parts of the question

▶ plan your answer carefully.

Comparative questions

Sometimes a question will ask you to compare. The questions on poetry will usually ask you to compare two or more poems but you might be also be asked to compare characters or settings, for example, within a text. Ensure you:

▶ read and understand what the question asks you to do

▶ compare the texts or features that you have been asked about

▶ plan your answer carefully.

WHAT MAKES AN A/A*, B OR C GRADE CANDIDATE

Obviously, you want to get the highest grade that you possibly can. The way to do this is to make sure that you have a good understanding of the texts that you study and are able to express your ideas on them in a clear, structured and fluent way.

GRADE A* ANSWER

The specification identifies what an A, C and F candidate can do in general terms. Examiners have to interpret these criteria when they fix grade boundaries. Boundaries are not fixed at the same mark every year and there is not a fixed percentage who achieve a particular grade each year. Boundaries are fixed by looking at candidates' work and comparing the standards with candidates of previous years. If the paper is harder than usual, the boundary mark will go down. The A* boundary is fixed initially at the same number of marks above the A boundary as the B is below it.

GRADE A ANSWER

A grade candidates can respond critically and sensitively to a range of texts, taking into account alternative approaches and interpretations. They explore and evaluate the ways meanings, ideas and feelings are conveyed through language, structure and form, making connections and comparisons between texts. They identify and comment on social, historical and cultural contexts of texts, and show awareness of literary tradition. They select forms appropriately and convey their ideas coherently.

GRADE B ANSWER

B grade candidates are able to analyse and appreciate the ways in which language is used in the texts studied and can select textual evidence appropriately to support personal and analytical response. They show an awareness of all aspects of the texts studied and analyse the contexts of texts appropriately, making connections and comparisons between them where required. They are also able to write accurately and communicate their ideas fluently and effectively.

GRADE C ANSWER

C grade candidates show understanding of how meanings and ideas are conveyed through language, structure and form. They explore connections and comparisons between texts, referring to details to support their views. They show awareness of some of the cultural and social contexts of texts. They convey their ideas appropriately in a range of forms.

 If you are likely to get a grade C or D on Higher tier, you would be seriously advised to take Foundation tier papers. You will find it easier to get your C on Foundation tier as you will not have to answer the questions targeted at A and B.

HOW TO BOOST YOUR GRADE

Grade booster ····⟩ How to turn C into B

- Know your texts in detail.
- Have plenty of ideas about them.
- Focus closely on what the question asks you to do – and do it.
- Cover a range of points and ideas.
- Support the points you make with accurate references to the text or short quotations from it.
- Plan your work carefully before you start to write.
- Examine and evaluate ideas.
- Analyse perceptively comparisons and relationships between texts.
- Structure your answer in a logical way, making sure that you write in sentences and paragraphs.
- Write fluently and accurately.
- Show independent understanding and appreciation of the different meanings and interpretations of the texts you study.
- Discuss the texts in detail showing awareness of the writers' intentions, attitudes and ideas.
- Your responses should show insight and your ability to explore your own thoughts and feelings about the texts you study.
- Be aware of the social and historical settings, cultural contexts and literary traditions of the texts you study.

Grade booster ····⟩ How to turn B into A/A*

- Know your texts in as much depth and detail as possible.
- Show insight into the ways in which language is used in the texts to create particular effects.
- Analyse the ways in which language is used and why writers have written in a particular way.
- Show an appreciation of the use of tone and vocabulary.
- Support your ideas with well-chosen textual references.
- Show a sustained analysis and evaluation of comparisons and relationships between texts.
- Structure your answer in a logical, clear and effective way.
- Write accurately and fluently.
- Your responses should be sustained and contain detailed evidence from the texts.
- They should contain enthusiastic personal responses.
- Your interpretations should be sophisticated and contain concise textual analysis.
- Your responses should show some originality of analysis and interpretation when evaluating the social and historical settings of texts, their cultural contexts or the literary traditions they draw on.

CHAPTER 1

Pre-1914 prose texts

See also Chapter 9 in Letts *Revise GCSE English and English Literature*.

Try this sample GCSE question and then compare your answer with the Grade C and Grade A model answers on pages 10 to 12.

Hard Times by Charles Dickens

Spend about 40 minutes on this.

Leave enough time to read through and correct what you have written.

The following passage comes from the opening of Chapter 2 of the novel.

Read it through carefully.

How does Dickens present Mr Gradgrind here?

How is this character important in the novel as a whole?

THOMAS GRADGRIND, sir. A man of realities. A man of fact and calculations. A man who proceeds upon the principle that two and two are four, and nothing over, and who is not to be talked into allowing for anything over. Thomas Gradgrind, sir – peremptorily Thomas – Thomas Gradgrind. With a rule and a pair of scales, and the multiplication table always in his pocket, sir, ready to weigh and measure any parcel of human nature, and tell you exactly what it comes to. It is a mere question of figures, a case of simple arithmetic. You might hope to get some other nonsensical belief into the head of George Gradgrind, or Augustus Gradgrind, or John Gradgrind, or Joseph Gradgrind (all supposititious, non-existent persons), but into the head of Thomas Gradgrind – no, sir!

In such terms Mr Gradgrind always mentally introduced himself, whether to his private circle of acquaintance, or to the public in general. In such terms, no doubt, substituting the words 'boys and girls' for 'sir', Thomas Gradgrind now presented Thomas Gradgrind to the little pitchers before him, who were to be filled so full of facts.

Indeed, as he eagerly sparkled at them from the cellarage before mentioned, he seemed a kind of cannon loaded to the muzzle with facts, and prepared to blow them clean out of the regions of childhood at one discharge. He seemed a galvanizing apparatus, too, charged with a grim mechanical substitute for the tender young imaginations that were to be stormed away.

'Girl number twenty,' said Mr Gradgrind, squarely pointing with his square forefinger, 'I don't know that girl. Who is that girl?'

'Sissy Jupe, sir,' explained number twenty, blushing, standing up, and curtseying.

'Sissy is not a name,' said Mr Gradgrind. 'Don't call yourself Sissy. Call yourself Cecilia.'

'It's father as calls me Sissy, sir,' returned the young girl in a trembling voice, and with another curtsey.

'Then he has no business to do it,' said Mr Gradgrind. 'Tell him he mustn't. Cecilia Jupe. Let me see. What is your father?'

'He belongs to the horse-riding, if you please, sir.'

Mr Gradgrind frowned, and waved off the objectionable calling with his hand.

'We don't want to know anything about that, here. You mustn't tell us about that, here. Your father breaks horses, don't he?'

'If you please, sir, when they can get any to break, they do break horses in the ring, sir.'

'You mustn't tell us about the ring, here. Very well, then. Describe your father as a horsebreaker. He doctors sick horses, I dare say?'

'Oh yes, sir.'

'Very well, then. He is a veterinary surgeon, a farrier and a horsebreaker. Give me your definition of a horse.'

(Sissy Jupe thrown into the greatest alarm by this demand.)

'Girl number twenty unable to define a horse!' said Mr Gradgrind, for the general behoof of all the little pitchers. 'Girl number twenty possessed of no facts, in reference to one of the commonest of animals! Some boy's definition of a horse. Bitzer, yours.'

The square finger, moving here and there, lighted suddenly on Bitzer, perhaps because he chanced to sit in the same ray of sunlight which, darting in at one of the bare windows of the intensely whitewashed room, irradiated Sissy. For, the boys and girls sat on the face of the inclined plane in two compact bodies, divided up the centre by a narrow interval; and Sissy, being at the corner of a row on the sunny side, came in for the beginning of a sunbeam, of which Bitzer, being at the corner of a row on the other side, a few rows in advance, caught the end. But, whereas the girl was so dark-eyed and dark-haired, that she seemed to receive a deeper and more lustrous colour from the sun when it shone upon her, the boy was so light-eyed and light-haired that the self-same rays appeared to draw out of him what little colour he ever possessed. His cold eyes would hardly have been eyes, but for the short ends of lashes which, by bringing them into immediate contrast with something paler than themselves, expressed their form. His short-cropped hair might have been a mere continuation of the sandy freckles on his forehead and face. His skin was so unwholesomely deficient in the natural tinge that he looked as though, if he were cut, he would bleed white.

'Bitzer,' said Thomas Gradgrind. 'Your definition of a horse.'

'Quadruped. Graminivorous. Forty teeth, namely twenty-four grinders, four eye-teeth, and twelve incisive. Sheds coat in the spring; in marshy countries, shed hoofs, too. Hoofs hard, but requiring to be shod with iron. Age known by marks in mouth.' Thus (and much more) Bitzer.

'Now girl number twenty,' said Mr Gradgrind. 'you know what a horse is.'

These two answers are at grades C and A. Compare them with your answer and think about how you might have improved your own response.

GRADE C ANSWER

Good assessment.

Good point supported by sound quotation.

Clear ideas on education and good support.

Shows a clear understanding of Gradgrind's attitude to imagination and to Sissy and what she represents for him.

Shows understanding of the relevance of Bitzer's definition of a horse and why Gradgrind approves of it.

Sound evaluation.

Reference to the importance to the novel but could be developed more.

SPELLCHECK!

severe
beginning
definite
doesn't

Sonia

Gradgrind is presented in the passage as a cold-hearted and sever kind of man. ✓ We are told at the beggining that he is a man who is only intrested in facts and nothing more. He thinks that everything should be definate and he applies these ideas even to people. For example, he calls Sissy 'Girl number twenty' ✓ which makes her sound more like a some kind of item than a human being.

He is a teacher but he has a particular idea that he uses in all his teaching. This idea involves only dealing with factual information and so he sees his students as little jugs that he has to fill up with facts ✓ – 'the little pitchers before him, who were to be filled so full of facts'.

He dosen't seem to be the kind of man who is very keen on imaginative ideas and who does not seem to like the idea of the circus. When Sissy talks about 'the ring' he tells her that she must not 'tell us about the ring here'. This is because the circus is to do with the imagination and not facts. ✓ Sissy seems to be frightened of him and when he tells her to define a horse she doesn't know what to say. Instead Gradgrind tells Bitzer to give his definition of a horse. Bitzer's definition only gives facts. ✓ 'Quadruped. Graminivorous. Forty teeth' and so on. It is obvious that Gradgrind likes this definition because it is a factual one and so when Bitzer has finished Gradgrind says to Sissy 'Now girl number twenty you know what a horse is'. Sissy already knew what a horse was because her father trained them in the circus. Overall then, in this passage, Gradgrind seems a cold, man who treats his students like objects rather than humans. He is obsessed with facts and dosen't want to know about anything else. ✓

He is an important character in the novel because he stands for ideas to do with facts and Dickens shows these to be in conflict with ideas of the imagination which is an important theme in the novel. ✓ Dickens uses him to show a wrong approach to education. We can see this because later in the novel Gradgrind realises that he is wrong and he changes and becomes much more human.

15/25

Grade booster ┈┈> move C to B

- More detailed exploration of ideas needed.
- The importance of Gradgrind in the novel as a whole could be developed.
- Technical accuracy needs attention.

GRADE A ANSWER

Mark

Doesn't really explain the point.

This passage is set in the whitewashed schoolroom and in many ways this room reflects what is going on in it and the attitude of the teacher, Mr. Gradgrind. The children who are being taught by Gradgrind are described as 'pitchers' who are being 'stuffed...full to the brim with facts.' This gives the impression that Gradgrind is interested only in teaching the students 'Facts'.

Sound assessment of Gradgrind.

✓ This idea is emphasised at the opening of the passage where Gradgrind is described as 'A man of realities. A man of fact and calculations.' ✓ This gives a very strong impression of a man for whom the sole basis for both education and life itself is 'Facts'.

Idea repeated and supported by use of some appropriate quotation.

This impression of the character is emphasised by Dickens' use of symbols to reflect his precise and factual nature:

'With a rule and a pair of scales, and the multiplication table always in his pocket, sir, ready to weigh and measure any parcel of human nature, and tell you exactly what it comes to.'

Very good point developed here and supported with accurate quotation and perceptive comments.

The image created through these precise measuring instruments emphasises the fact that he believes everything can be precisely weighed and measured – even human nature. ✓ His nature is even reflected in his name – Gradgrind. ✓

It seems that to Gradgrind 'imagination' is something undesirable to be driven out of children. This idea can be seen in his questioning of Sissy. The very fact that he refers to her as 'Girl number twenty' shows his precise nature – it is efficient to number people but it also takes away their individuality in some way. ✓ He even goes so far as to say that her father should not call her Sissy because it '...is not a name.'

Close focus and development of ideas.

His feelings are further shown when he tells Sissy to define a horse. She is so alarmed by this that she cannot do it so Gradgrind announces that 'Girl number twenty possessed of no facts, in reference to one of the commonest animals'. ✓ He then turns to Bitzer and tells him to define a horse. Bitzer gives a completely factual definition:

Evaluation of Sissy's feelings and Gradgrind's attitude.

'Quadruped. Graminivorous. Forty teeth, namely twenty-four grinders, four eye-teeth, and twelve incisive. Sheds coat in the spring; in marshy countries, shed hoofs, too.'

Clear awareness shown of the significance of Bitzer's definition and to the wider historical/social context and the values that Dickens is criticising.

Gradgrind is obviously approving of this definition because it is completely factual. ✓ This again serves to emphasise how Gradgrind's philosophy is based on 'Facts'. As his life centres on facts he shows no emotion in this extract and seems cold and unfeeling which is probably the impression he wants to create because he is being critical of the utilitarian attitudes that some people had in the nineteenth century.

Some focus on the rest of the novel but quite brief. This could be developed further.

Gradgrind is important in the novel as a whole because through him Dickens explores how his beliefs actually work out in practice. We see this through the effects these beliefs have on his own children, Tom and Louisa. As you might expect, his ideas are shown to fail because these are the ideas that Dickens is criticising. By the end of the novel his ideas are shown to be completely wrong and he himself is shown to change and to develop a new-found faith in human feelings and the imagination. ✓ In this sense, then, Gradgrind is important to the novel as a whole because he is at the centre of the debate that Dickens develops of the conflict between the 'wisdom of the head' and the 'wisdom of the heart'.

22/25

Grade booster ⋯⋯⟩ move A to A*

More detailed attention could be given to an examination of Gradgrind's importance in the novel as whole.

Spend about 45 minutes on each question in this section. Each question carries **25 marks**.

Wuthering Heights **by Emily Bronte**

1 Hindley describes Heathcliff as a 'fiend' and a 'hellish villain' and Isabella comments that he appears an 'incarnate goblin', 'a monster and not a human being'.

What is your view of the presentation of the character of Heathcliff in *Wuthering Heights*?

2 What does the wild and rugged setting of *Wuthering Heights* add to the novel?

3 What is the importance of Nelly Dean and Joseph in *Wuthering Heights*?

4 This passage is taken from the end of *Wuthering Heights*.

We buried him, to the scandal of the whole neighbourhood, as he had wished. Earnshaw, and I, the sexton and six men to carry the coffin, comprehended the whole attendance. The six men departed when they had let it down into the grave: we stayed to see it covered. Hareton, with a streaming face, dug green sods, and laid them over the brown mound himself: at present it is as smooth and verdant as its companion mounds – and I hope its tenant sleeps as soundly. But the country folks, if you asked them, would swear on their bible that he *walks*. There are those who speak to having met him near the church, and on the moor, and even within this house. Idle tales, you'll say, and so say I. Yet that old man by the kitchen fire affirms he has seen two on 'em looking out of his chamber window, on every rainy night since his death: – and an odd thing happened to me about a month ago. I was going to the Grange one evening – a dark evening threatening thunder – and, just at the turn of the Heights, I encountered a little boy with a sheep and two lambs before him; he was crying terribly, and I supposed the lambs were skittish, and would not be guided.

'What is the matter, my little man:' I asked.

'There's Heathcliff, and a woman, yonder, under t' Nab', he blubbered, 'un' I darnut pass 'em.'

I saw nothing; but either the sheep nor he would go on: so I bid him take the road lower down. He probably raised the phantoms from thinking, as he traversed the moors alone, on the nonsense he had heard his parents and companions repeat – yet still, I don't like being out in the dark, now; and I don't like being left by myself in this grim house: I cannot help it; I shall be glad when they leave it, and shift to the Grange.

'They are going to the Grange then?' I said.

'Yes,' answered Mrs. Dean, 'as soon as they are married, and that will be on New Year's day.'

'And who will live here then?'

'Why, Joseph will take care of the house, and, perhaps, a lad to keep him company. They will live in the kitchen, and the rest will be shut up.'

'For the use of such ghosts as choose to inhabit it,' I observed.

'No, Mr. Lockwood,' said Nelly, shaking her head. 'I believe the dead are at peace: but it is not right to speak of them with levity.'

At that moment the garden gate swung to; the ramblers were returning.

'*They* are afraid of nothing,' I grumbled, watching their approach through the window. 'Together, they would brave Satan and all his legions.'

As they stepped on to the door-stones, and halted to take a last look at the moon – or, more correctly, at each other, by her light – I felt irresistibly impelled to escape them again; and, pressing a remembrance into the hand of Mrs. Dean, and disregarding her expostulations at my rudeness, I vanished through the kitchen as they opened the house-door; and so should have confirmed Joseph in his opinion of his fellow-servant's gay indiscretions, had he not fortunately recognised me for a respectable character by the sweet ring of a sovereign at his feet.

My walk home was lengthened by a diversion in the direction of the kirk. When beneath its walls, I perceived decay had made progress, even in seven months: many a window showed black gaps deprived of glass; and slates jutted off, here and there, beyond the right line of the roof, to be gradually worked off in coming autumn storms.

I sought, and soon discovered, the three headstones on the slope next the moor: the middle one grey, and half buried in heath; Edgar Linton's only harmonised by the turf, and moss creeping up its foot; Heathcliff's still bare.

I lingered round them, under that benign sky: watched the moths fluttering among the heath and harebells' listened to the soft wind breathing through the grass; and wondered how anyone could ever imagine unquiet slumbers for the sleepers in that quiet earth.

How effective do you find the ending of the novel?

Hard Times by Charles Dickens

1 The following description of Coketown is taken from the beginning of Chapter 5.

Coketown, to which Messrs Bounderby and Gradgrind now walked, was a triumph of fact; it had no greater taint of fancy in it than Mrs Gradgrind herself. Let us strike the key-note, Coketown, before pursuing our tune.

It was a town of red brick, or of brick that would have been red if the smoke and ashes had allowed it; but, as matters stood it was a town of unnatural red and black like the painted face of a savage.

It was a town of machinery and tall chimneys, out of which interminable serpents of smoke trailed themselves for ever and ever, and never got uncoiled.

It had a black canal in it, and a river that ran purple with ill-smelling dye, and vast piles of building full of windows where there was a rattling and a trembling all day long, and where the piston of the steam-engine worked monotonously up and down, like the head of an elephant in a state of melancholy madness. It contained several large streets all very like one another, and many small streets still more like one another, inhabited by people equally like one another, who all went in and out at the same hours, with the same sound upon the same pavements, to do the same work, and to whom every day was the same as yesterday and tomorrow, and every year the counterpart of the last and the next.

These attributes of Coketown were in the main inseparable from the work by which it was sustained; against them were to be set off, comforts of life which found their way all over the world, and elegancies of life which made, we will not ask how much of the fine lady, who could scarcely bear to hear the place mentioned. The rest of its features were voluntary, and they were these.

You saw nothing in Coketown but what was severely workful. If the members of a religious persuasion had done – they made it a pious warehouse of red brick, with sometimes (but this only in highly ornamented examples) a bell in a bird-cage on the top of it. The solitary exception was the New Church; a stuccoed edifice with a square steeple over the door, terminating in four short pinnacles like florid wooden legs. All the public inscriptions in the town were painted alike, in severe characters of black and white. The jail might have been the infirmary, the infirmary might have been the jail, the town-hall might have been either, or both, or anything else, for anything that appeared to the contrary in the graces of their construction. Fact, fact, fact, everywhere in the material aspect of the town; fact, fact, fact, everywhere in the immaterial. The M'Choakumchild school was all fact, and the school of design was all fact, and the relations between master and man were all fact, and everything was fact between the lying-in-hospital and the cemetery, and what you couldn't state in figures, or show to be purchasable in the cheapest market and saleable in the dearest, was not, and never should be, world without end, Amen.

How does Dickens present Coketown here? How does this setting add to the overall effect of the novel?

2 How does Dickens explore the theme of education in *Hard Times*?

You should write about:

- Mr Gradgrind
- Louisa and Tom
- Bitzer and Sissy
- any other ideas of your own.

3 Write about the importance of three of the following characters in *Hard Times*:

a) Sissy Jupe

b) Bitzer

c) Josiah Bounderby

d) Stephen Blackpool

4 What is the importance of the circus in *Hard Times?*

Silas Marner by George Eliot

1 What do you think Silas Marner has to say about human nature?

2 Compare the characters of Godfrey Cass and Silas Marner.

3 Remind yourself of Chapter 11 where George Eliot draws together various members of the community. How does Eliot present her characters here and what is the importance of this section to the novel as a whole?

4 In this passage near the beginning of Chapter 3, Eliot describes Dunstan Cass.

> Raveloe was not a place where moral censure was severe, but it was thought a weakness in the Squire that he had kept all his sons at home in idleness; and though some licence was to be allowed to young men whose fathers could afford it, people shook their heads at the courses of the second son, Dunstan, commonly called Dunsey Cass, whose taste for swopping and betting might turn out to be a sowing of something worse than wild oats. To be sure, the neighbours said, it was no matter what became of Dunsey – a spiteful jeering fellow, who seemed to enjoy his drink the more when other people went dry – always provided that his doings did not bring trouble on a family like Squire Cass's, with a monument in the church, and tankards older than King George.

How does Eliot present Dunstan Cass here and elsewhere in the novel?

5 Examine Eliot's portrayal of women in *Silas Marner*.

Write about three of the following:

- Nancy Lammeter
- Eppie
- Priscilla Lammeter
- Dolly Winthrop.

Pride and Prejudice by Jane Austen

1 This extract is taken from the opening of the novel.

> It is a truth universally acknowledged, that a single man in possession of a good fortune, must be in want of a wife.
>
> However little known the feelings or views of such a man may be on his first entering a neighbourhood, this truth is so well fixed in the minds of the surrounding families, that he is considered as the rightful property of some one or other of their daughters.
>
> 'My dear Mr. Bennet,' said his lady to him one day, 'have you heard that Netherfield Park is let at last?'
>
> Mr. Bennet replied that he had not.
>
> 'But it is,' returned she; 'for Mrs. Long has just been here, and she told me all about it.'
>
> Mr. Bennet made no answer.
>
> 'Do not you want to know who has taken it?' cried his wife impatiently.

'*You* want to tell me, and I have no objection to hearing it.'

This was invitation enough.

'Why, my dear, you must know, Mrs. Long says that Netherfield is taken by a young man of large fortune from the north of England; that he came down on Monday in a chaise and four to see the place, and was so much delighted with it that he agreed with Mr. Morris immediately; that he is to take possession before Michaelmas, and some of his servants are to be in the house by the end of next week.'

'What is his name?'

'Bingley.'

Is he married or single?'

'Oh! single, my dear, to be sure! A single man of large fortune; four or five thousand a year. What a fine thing for our girls!'

'How so? How can it affect them?'

'My dear Mr. Bennet,' replied his wife, 'how can you be so tiresome! You must know that I am thinking of his marrying one of them.'

'Is that his design in settling here?'

'Design! nonsense, how can you talk so? But it is very likely that he may fall in love with one of them, and therefore you must visit him as soon as he comes.'

How does this opening introduce a central theme of the novel?

---

2 What different kinds of marriages does Austen present in the novel? Do you think she presents one kind of marriage in a more favourable light than the others?

Write about:

- Charlotte's marriage to Collins
- Lydia's marriage to Wickham
- Elizabeth's marriage to Darcy.

---

3 How are 'pride' and 'prejudice' important in the novel?

How well-matched do you think Elizabeth and Darcy, and Jane and Bingley are?

---

4 Examine the relationship between Elizabeth and Darcy. Compare this relationship with that between Jane and Bingley.

Far From the Madding Crowd by Thomas Hardy

1 How does Hardy present the character of Bathsheba Everdene? Do you think her character changes during the course of the novel?

---

2 What is the role of nature in the novel? Write about:

- the storm
- the fire
- any other aspects of nature you find important.

3 This passage is taken from Chapter 28 and describes Troy displaying his swordmanship to Bathsheba.

In an instant the atmosphere was transformed to Bathsheba's eyes. Beams of light caught from the low sun's rays, above, around, in front of her, well-nigh shut out earth and heaven – all emitted in the marvellous evolutions of Troy's reflecting blade, which seemed everywhere at once, and yet nowhere specially. These circling gleams were accompanied by a keen rush that was almost a whistling – also springing from all sides of her at once. In short, she was enclosed in a firmament of light, and of sharp hisses, resembling a sky-full of meteors close at hand.

Never since the broadsword became the national weapon had there been more dexterity shown in its management than by the hands of Sergeant Troy, and never had he been in such splendid temper for the performance as now in the evening sunshine among the ferns with Bathsheba. It may safely be asserted with respect to the closeness of his cuts, that had it been possible for the edge of the sword to leave in the air a permanent substance wherever it flew past, the space left untouched would have been almost a mould of Bathsheba's figure.

Behind the luminous streams of this *aurora militaris*, she could see the hue of Troy's sword arm, spread in a scarlet haze over the space covered by its motions, like a twanged harpstring, and behind all Troy himself, mostly facing her; sometimes, to show the rear cuts, half turned away, his eye nevertheless always keenly measuring her breadth and outline, and his lips tightly closed in sustained effort. Next, his movements lapsed slower, and she could see them individually. The hissing of the sword had ceased, and he stopped entirely.

'That outer loose lock of hair wants tidying,' he said, before she had moved or spoken. 'Wait: I'll do it for you.'

An arc of silver shone on her right side: the sword had descended. The lock dropped to the ground.

'Bravely borne!' said Troy. 'You didn't flinch a shade's thickness. Wonderful in a woman!'

'It was because I didn't expect it. O, you have spoilt my hair!'

'Only once more.'

'No – no! I am afraid of you – indeed I am!' she cried.

'I won't touch you at all – not even your hair. I am only going to kill that caterpillar settling on you. Now: still!'

It appeared that a caterpillar had come from the fern and chosen the front of her bodice as his resting place. She saw the point glisten towards her bosom, and seemingly enter it. Bathsheba closed her eyes in the full persuasion that she was killed at last. However, feeling just as usual, she opened them again.

'There it is, look,' said the sergeant, holding his sword before her eyes.

The caterpillar was spitted upon its point.

'Why, it is magic!' said Bathsheba amazed.

How is Sergeant Troy presented both here and elsewhere in the novel?

4 Remind yourself of the storm scene in Chapter 37.

What does the scene reveal about the character of Gabriel Oak? How are these aspects reflected elsewhere in the novel?

QUESTION BANK ANSWERS

EXAMINER'S TIP

Literary texts can be open to more than one interpretation and questions do not necessarily have 'right' or 'wrong' answers. They do want you to explore your ideas though and support those ideas with references to the texts. The points given here are suggested ideas you might explore but do not present the only ideas that you might include in an answer.

Wuthering Heights

① Here are some ideas.
- Heathcliff can be seen as the embodiment of a dark force.
- Many references refer to his 'dark' aspects and images link him to evil and the devil.
- Other descriptions present a fierce, heartless and pitiless man.
- He is badly treated as a child by Hindley, though, and this gives rise to his desire for vengeance.
- His love for Catherine possesses him entirely.

② Here are some ideas.
- There is a constant emphasis on the landscape, which takes on a symbolic importance.
- The wild moors cannot be cultivated and are dark and threatening.
- This creates a sombre mood, which is in keeping with the character of Heathcliff.
- The wildness of the moors also represents the unbounded passion that Heathcliff feels for Cathy – the moorland also provides the backdrop to their love affair.

EXAMINER'S TIP

When writing about characters think about:
- *what they do*
- *what they say*
- *what others say about them*
- *their relationship with other characters*
- *the ways in which the writer uses language to describe and present them.*

③ Here are some ideas.
Nelly
- She is the chief narrator of the story.
- She is presented as a sensible and compassionate woman.
- She is deeply involved with the characters and the story she tells as she saw them grow up.

Joseph
- He adds to the sense of hostility at Wuthering Heights.
- His speech, with his strong Yorkshire accent, emphasises the sense of wildness and alien nature of the place as seen through Lockwood's eyes.
- He is God fearing – often quoting the Bible. This sets him in contrast with Heathcliff.

④ Here are some ideas.
- This kind of question invites you to give your own views on the effectiveness of the ending.
- You can argue your case either way as long as you support and justify the ideas you put forward.

EXAMINER'S TIP

Remember to focus on specific details from the text to support the points that you make.

Hard Times

① Here are some ideas.
- The description emphasises some of the points made in the earlier chapters.
- The town is completely given over to the factory system.
- The mechanical nature of the place is reflected in its architecture and layout.
- The whole place is devoid of individuality and is repetitive.
- Even the people are 'machine-like'.

EXAMINER'S TIP

The setting or context of a novel is important and often is linked to the themes and ideas explored.

② Here are some ideas.
- Gradgrind's educational methods are based completely on facts and not imagination.
- The novel presents how a utilitarian approach to education can be damaging to individual development.
- Louisa and Tom are guinea pigs for Gradgrind's experiment on raising the young only on facts.
- Bitzer and Sissy represent the opposite ends of the scale – Bitzer has been brought up only on facts and is devoid of feelings; Sissy has been exposed to a world of the imagination and has wisdom and a strong moral sense.

❸ Here are some ideas.
  • Sissy represents the importance of the imagination over facts.
  • Bitzer is the perfect product of the Gradgrind educational system and has no feelings for other people.
  • Bounderby links the two main themes of the novel – the educational and the industrial.
  • Stephen Blackpool is typical of his class – a skilled but badly paid factory worker. He is a victim of the system but a man of complete integrity.

❹ Here are some ideas.
  • The circus represents the world of the imagination.
  • It forms a complete contrast with the world of Coketown, the school, and Gradgrind
  • The circus animals, who are important in the outwitting of Bitzer, represent instinct – the opposite of the calculated behaviour represented by Gradgrind.
  • Sleary's philosophy forms a contrast to Gradgrind's philosophy.

Silas Marner
❶ Here are some ideas.
  • The novel explores how human relationships can breathe new life into an individual.
  • Love and kindness can help to restore faith in humanity.
  • A community can provide a structure and sense of identity to its members.
  • Sin is punished and goodness rewarded.

❷ Here are some ideas.
  Silas Marner
  • Although reclusive, he is kind and honest.
  • He loves money because he has nothing else in his life.
  • He is passive – things happen to him rather than him shaping events but, in the end, his actions bring about good.
  • He shows love and sacrifice when he takes in and raises Eppie.

  Godfrey Cass
  • He is good-natured but weak-willed.
  • He thinks about little beyond his immediate needs and comfort.
  • He shows guilt and moral cowardice.
  • Like Silas, he is mainly passive but he is different because it stems mainly from selfishness.

❸ Here are some ideas.
  • Eliot creates a sense of the community by bringing them all together here.
  • All classes and ages are represented and we gain insights into what kinds of people they are.

  • The others comment on the way Nancy speaks.
  • There is a contrast between the characters of Nancy and Godfrey.
  • Nancy sticks to her principles.
  • Godfrey lacks self-control.
  • In contrast to them both, Priscilla Lammeter stands out as being honest and straightforward.

❹ Here are some ideas.
  • He is presented here as an unpleasant spiteful character.
  • He likes to drink.
  • He does not care about others.
  • In the novel as a whole he is presented as greedy and cruel.
  • He enjoys tormenting Godfrey.
  • He blackmails Godfrey.
  • He steals Silas's money.

❺ Here are some ideas.
  • Nancy is pretty, caring and stubborn and she has strict values.
  • Eppie grows up loyal to Silas and with a feeling and awareness of the needs of others.
  • Priscilla accepts her position in life but does not conform to conventional feminine manners and behaviour.
  • Dolly is a devout Christian and is always ready to help others, as she does Silas in bringing up Eppie.

EXAMINER'S TIP

▶▶ *Make sure you support the points you make with references to the text and short but relevant quotations where appropriate.*

Pride and Prejudice
❶ Here are some ideas.
  • This opening introduces the arrival of Mr Bingley at Netherfield, which is the event that sets the whole novel in motion.
  • This opening also sketches out the central idea of the whole plot, which concerns itself with the pursuit of 'single men in possession of a good fortune' by the various female characters in the novel.
  • This, in turn, touches upon the preoccupation amongst the higher ranks of nineteenth-century society with trying to achieve socially advantageous marriages.

EXAMINER'S TIP

▶▶ *Be aware of the themes and ideas in the texts that you study.*

❷ Here are some ideas.
  • Charlotte marries Mr Collins for his money, which demonstrates that the heart does not always dictate marriage.

- Darcy and Elizabeth, despite the various stumbling blocks that they have to overcome, marry for love.
- Lydia's elopement with Wickham, and living with him as his lover without the benefit of marriage, places Lydia outside what is socially accepted and brings disgrace on the family.
- Each of these relationships presents different kinds of love or different ways that the idea of love is used as a means of social advancement.

❸ Here are some ideas.
- The words 'pride' and 'prejudice' embody the key themes of the novel.
- Darcy's pride leads him to be viewed as arrogant by Elizabeth and other characters.
- Elizabeth also shows a pride that stands in the way of her developing a relationship with Darcy.
- Prejudice often leads characters to form false impressions of others.
- It is only when Darcy puts aside his pride and Elizabeth becomes more accepting that they find happiness together.

❹ Here are some ideas.
- Elizabeth is an intelligent, witty and vivacious young lady who is not afraid to speak her mind.
- She is honest, to both herself and others and, once she realises the truth about Darcy, she admits that she has been wrong and prejudiced against him and is sorry that she rejected him.
- Darcy, in return, asks her to marry him and his pride, which was one of the barriers that stood between them, is put aside.
- In the end, their love is sincere and the two are well matched.
- Jane and Bingley are well matched.
- They are both gentle and amiable and are attracted to each other immediately.
- Unlike Darcy and Elizabeth, who initially have difficulties in understanding each other, Jane and Bingley have no such difficulties of communication.

Far From the Madding Crowd
❶ Here are some ideas.
- Bathsheba is a high-spirited and capricious character.
- She is independent and practical and is reluctant to accept help from others.
- She is a young woman and can act impetuously as she does in sending the valentine card to Farmer Boldwood.
- She likes to be admired and flattered and so is easily taken in by the charms of Sergeant Troy.

- Throughout the course of the novel, she matures and begins to be genuinely concerned with other people and this is reflected in her changed attitude towards Gabriel.

❷ Here are some ideas.
- Nature is presented as a harsh and unrelenting force.
- This can be seen through the description of the storm that threatens Bathsheba's crops.
- It can also be seen in the death of Gabriel's lambs.
- The fire also shows the destructive force of nature.
- Nature is also presented in more benevolent forms, such as in the descriptions of the warm spring nights and summer days spent washing and shearing.
- Hardy often focuses on small details of natural description, such as the buttercups that stain Boldwood's boots as he walks through the field.

❸ Here are some ideas.
- In the passage, we see Troy in a dashing and exciting light.
- The expert swordplay of the soldier, which he shows here, achieves his desired effect of captivating and impressing Bathsheba.
- Elsewhere in the novel, though, he is revealed as a constantly restless character who is never satisfied with what he has.
- In this sense, although exciting and attractive, he is also rather shallow and empty.
- He feels free to lie to women.
- Like Bathsheba, he shows an independent nature but, unlike her, he doesn't mature as a character during the course of the novel.
- He enjoys being master of the farm but shows little concern for the well-being of his workers or for working himself.

❹ Here are some ideas.
- It is Gabriel who is aware of the effect of the lightning on the countryside and realises the danger in being on top of the haystack.
- Before the rain has started, he is concerned about the coming storm and is worried about the harvest.
- He helps Bathsheba – both are on the hayrick when it is struck by lightning but both are saved by Gabriel's forethought in attaching an earth to the ground.
- He defends the others who are asleep in the barn.
- His faithfulness to Bathsheba is seen here and elsewhere in the novel.

CHAPTER 2

Post-1914 prose texts

See also Chapter 9 in Letts *Revise GCSE English and English Literature*.

Try this sample GCSE question and then compare your answer with the Grade C and Grade A model answers on pages 24 to 26.

Of Mice and Men by John Steinbeck

Spend about 40 minutes on this.

Leave enough time to read through and correct what you have written.

The following passage from Chapter 2 describes Curley's wife and Lennie's reaction to her.

> Both men glanced up, for the rectangle of sunshine in the doorway was cut off. A girl was standing there looking in. She had full, rouged lips and wide-spaced eyes, heavily made up. Her finger-nails were red. Her hair hung in little rolled clusters, like sausages. She wore a cotton house dress and red mules, on the insteps of which were little bouquets of red ostrich feathers. 'I'm lookin' for Curley,' she said. Her voice had a nasal, brittle quality.
>
> George looked away from her and then back. 'He was in here a minute ago, but he went.'
>
> 'Oh!' She put her hands behind her back and leaned against the door-frame so that her body was thrown forward. 'You're the new fellas that just come, ain't ya?'
>
> 'Yeah.'
>
> Lennie's eyes moved down over her body, and although she did not seem to be looking at Lennie, she bridled a little. She looked at her finger-nails. 'Sometimes Curley's in here,' she explained.
>
> George said brusquely: 'Well, he ain't now.'
>
> 'If he ain't, I guess I better look some place else,' she said playfully.
>
> Lennie watched her, fascinated. George said: 'If I see him, I'll pass the word you was looking for him.'

She smiled archly and twitched her body. 'Nobody can't blame a person for lookin',' she said. There were footsteps behind her, going by. She turned her head. 'Hi, Slim,' she said.

Slim's voice came through the door. 'Hi, Good-lookin'.'

'I'm trying to find Curley, Slim.'

'Well, you ain't tryin' very hard. I seen him goin' in your house.'

She was suddenly apprehensive. ''Bye, boys,' she called into the bunkhouse, and she hurried away.

George looked around at Lennie. 'Jesus, what a tramp,' he said. 'So that's what Curley picks for a wife.'

'She's purty,' said Lennie defensively.

'Yeah, and she's sure hidin' it. Curley got his work ahead of him. Bet she'd clear out for twenty bucks.'

Lennie still stared at the doorway where she had been. 'Gosh, she was purty.' He smiled admiringly. George looked quickly down at him and then he took him by an ear and shook him.

'Listen to me, you crazy bastard,' he said fiercely. 'Don't you even take a look at that bitch. I don't care what she says and what she does. I seen 'em poison before, but I never seen no piece of jail bait worse than her. You leave her be.'

Lennie tried to disengage his ear. 'I never done nothing, George.'

'No, you never. But when she was standin' in the doorway showin' her legs, you wasn't lookin' the other way, neither.'

'I never meant no harm, George. Honest I never.'

'Well, you keep away from her, 'cause she's a rat-trap if I ever seen one. You let Curley take the rap. He let himself in for it. Glove fulla vaseline,' George said disgustedly. 'An I bet he's eatin' raw eggs and writin' to the patent medicine houses.'

How does Steinbeck present Curley's wife in this passage?

What is the importance of Curley's wife in the novel as a whole?

These two answers are at grades C and A. Compare them with your answer and think about how you might have improved your own response.

GRADE C ANSWER

Wesley

Gives an evaluation based on description.

Avoid using slang.

Supporting quotation.

Personal response based on evidence. Focus on details of language.

Good use of quotation and some analytical comment.

Well-chosen supporting quotations.

Links to plot and importance of Curly's wife to later developments in plot.

Could be more clearly expressed.

Accurate summary but lacks development.

The passage opens as Curley's wife stands in the doorway looking in at the men. The way that Steinbeck describes her ✓ gives the impression of quite a tarty kind of woman:

'She had full, rouged lips and wide-spaced eyes, heavily made up. Her finger-nails were red.'

The way she is dressed makes you think this even more, especially her red sandals with little bunches of red ostrich feathers. This idea of red is often linked to 'lose women'. The way she moves also gives this kind of feeling in the way that she puts her hands behind her back and pushes her chest out.

George seems to have thought this because when she has gone he says 'Jesus, what a tramp'. ✓ By 'tramp' he means a tarty woman. This is different to what Lennie thinks though because he thinks that she is pretty. That's because he is inocent though and doesn't really see through her. He says this twice which really emphasies how taken with her he is. This makes George really mad and he calls Lennie a 'crazy bastard' and warns him 'Don't you even take a look at that bitch' and he calls her 'poison' and 'jail bait'. ✓

This is important because it sort of hints at what is to happen later in the book. She is important because she causes the problems at the end of the book. ✓ It is because Lennie likes her that he wants to pet her hair and when she panics he accidentally kills her. This is all inocent on Lennie's part but she thinks he is going to attack her but then she panics he doesn't understand what is going on. Really, though, it was her fault because she encouraged him to feel her but he got carried away and when she started to struggle and shout he tried to shut her up but not knowing his own strength he killed her:

'"Don't you go yellin'," he said, and he shook her; and he body flopped like a fish. And then she was still, for Lennie had broken her neck.'

She is important in the novel as a whole, then, because she is what brings about the whole tragdedy and in the end causes George to shoot Lennie. ✓

14/25

SPELLCHECK!

loose
innocent
emphasises
encouraged
tragedy

Grade booster ···> move C to B
- More detailed development of ideas needed.
- More focus needed on how Curly's wife is important to the novel as a whole.
- Technical accuracy needs attention.

Sophie

Curley's wife in the passage is very flirtatious. ✓ Although the scene that is set is the workman's hut on a working ranch, she appears dressed in a cotton house dress and red mules with red ostrich feathers on. ✓ She has red finger-nails; full, rouged lips and is heavily made up. Her body language also shows her flirtations. ✓ For example, the stance she takes is such that it throws her body forward, she smiles and twitches her body and she obviously knows what effect this is having: 'Although she did not seem to be looking at Lennie, she bridled a little.' ✓ She obviously went to the hut to seek male attention and not her husband. When she says she is looking for Curley, Slim states: 'You ain't tryin' very hard.' ✓ The difference in the characters Lennie and George is further emphasised in their reactions to her. Lennie is quite innocent in his observations: 'she's purty'. However, George, who is portrayed as being more astute, ✓ sees straight through Curley's wife's playful talk: 'She's a rat trap.'

However, George's description of her being a tramp appears to be a little unfair. She seeks male attention which suggests that she doesn't get much attention from her husband – this is evidently true as we see later in the play when we find out more about Curley's character. She is obviously a lonely, insecure woman ✓ and somewhat naïve if she thinks that the men actually believe that she is looking for her husband. The contrast between the flirtatiousness and naivety is further emphasised as, initially, even though she is dressed as a woman, she is described as being a girl.

A sense of foreboding is achieved in this passage which supports the conclusion of the novel. For instance, through George's advice to Lennie: 'Don't you even take a look...I never seen no piece of jail bait worse than her' ✓ and more subtly through her initial entry into the cabin: 'the rectangle of sunshine in the doorway was cut off... A girl was standing there looking in'. ✓ This introduces and supports the importance of Curley's wife in the novel. However, the character of Curley's wife is not just important because of her role in the novel's conclusion, her character supports some of the key themes contained within it. For example, the novel explores the theme of isolation ✓ through both its setting and characters such as Crooks. Curley's wife helps to support this as she appears not only isolated from other women by being in an all-male environment, but also from opportunities and experiences which would see her develop as a person.

Accurate assessment.

Good focus on details.

Close reading and good use of supporting quotation.

Good point showing contrast in characters.

Clear evaluation of the characters and very subtle and perceptive point here.

Effective use of quotation.

Good links with the themes of the novel.

Again good focus on wider themes and some close reading here.

An interesting and perceptive point well-made.

Summary re-emphasising the key themes.

The character of Curley's wife also supports the theme of 'dreams' ✓ evident in the novel. This theme is expressed mainly through George and Lennie's dream of their future, but Curley's wife too had a dream of being famous and unfortunately hers, like theirs, would never be realised. Again her naivety is evident here as she appears to believe that her dream could actually have come true, even though we are told that the man never intended to come back for her. Although, perhaps it is her fear of facing the truth, and not naivety, which causes her to believe this. ✓

Perhaps the most striking characteristic of Curley's wife is that she is given no name. ✓ This is an important omission and supports the idea of worthlessness that the character feels about herself, and which is felt of her by other characters – as George observes: 'Jesus, she's a tramp'. In this respect, the character of Curley's wife supports Steinbeck's presentation of human life as being valueless. ✓ His description and presentation of attitudes towards itinerant workers, people from other cultures, and older people expresses a harsh world of loneliness and isolation and, as these are themes captured in her, this is why the character of Curley's wife is so important in Of Mice and Men.

22/25

Grade booster ····⟩ move A to A*

Greater focus could be made on the role Curley's wife plays at the end of the novel in terms of bringing about the tragic ending.

Spend about 45 minutes on each question in this section. Each question carries **25 marks**.

Lord of the Flies

1 The following passage is taken from Chapter 1 where the boys vote for a chief.

There was a buzz. One of the small boys, Henry, said that he wanted to go home.

'Shut up,' said Ralph absently. He lifted the conch. 'Seems to me we ought to have a chief to decide things.'

'A chief! A chief!'

'I ought to be chief,' said Jack with simple arrogance, 'because I'm chapter chorister and head boy. I can sing C sharp.'

Another buzz.

'Well then,' said Jack, 'I–'

He hesitated. The dark boy, Roger, stirred at last and spoke up.

'Let's have a vote.'

'Yes!'

'Vote for a chief!'

This toy of voting was almost as pleasing as the conch. Jack started to protest but the clamour changed from the general wish for a chief to an election by acclaim of Ralph himself. None of the boys could have found good reason for this; what intelligence had been shown was traceable to Piggy while the most obvious leader was Jack. But there was a stillness about Ralph as he sat that marked him out: there was his size, and attractive appearance; and most obscurely, yet most powerfully, there was the conch. The being that had blown that, had sat waiting for them on the platform with the delicate thing balanced on his knees, was set apart.

'Him with the shell.'

'Ralph! Ralph!'

'Let him be chief with the trumpet-thing.'

Ralph raised a hand for silence.

'All right. Who wants Jack for chief?'

With dreary obedience the choir raised their hands.

'Who wants me?'

Every hand outside the choir except Piggy's was raised immediately. Then Piggy too, raised his hand grudgingly into the air.

Ralph counted.

'I'm chief then.'

The circle of boys broke into applause. Even the choir applauded; and the freckles on Jack's face disappeared under a blush of mortification. He started up, then changed his mind and sat down again while the air rang. Ralph looked at him eager to offer something.

'The choir belongs to you, of course.'

'They could be the army –'

'Or hunters –'

'They could be –'

The suffusion drained away from Jack's face. Ralph waved again for silence.

'Jack's in charge of the choir. They can be – what do you want them to be?'

'Hunters.'

How does Golding present Ralph and Jack in this passage?

How does this passage prepare us for what is to come later in the novel?

2 Read the last part of Chapter 2 again, 'Fire on the Mountain', where the boys have set fire to the forest.

'You got your small fire all right.'

Startled, Ralph realized that the boys were falling still and silent, feeling the beginnings of awe at the power set free below them. The knowledge and the awe made him savage.

'Oh, shut up!'

'I got the conch,' said Piggy, in a hurt voice. 'I got a right to speak.'

They looked at him with eyes that lacked interest in what they saw, and cocked ears at the drum-roll of the fire. Piggy glanced nervously into hell and cradled the conch.

'We got to let that burn out now. And that was our firewood.'

He licked his lips.

'There ain't nothing we can do. We ought to be more careful. I'm scared –'

Jack dragged his eyes away from the fire.

'You're always scared. Yah – Fatty!'

'I got the conch,' said Piggy bleakly. He turned to Ralph. 'I got the conch, ain't I Ralph?'

Unwillingly Ralph turned away from the splendid, awful sight.

'What's that?'

'The conch. I got a right to speak.'

The twins giggled together.

'We wanted smoke –'

'Now look –'

A pall stretched for miles away from the island. All the boys except Piggy started to giggle; presently they were shrieking with laughter.

Piggy lost his temper.

'I got the conch! Just you listen! The first thing we ought to have made was shelters down there by the beach. It wasn't half cold down there in the night. But the first time Ralph says 'fire' you goes howling and screaming up this here mountain. Like a pack of kids!'

By now they were listening to the tirade.

'How can you expect to be rescued if you don't put first things first and act proper?'

He took off his glasses and made as if to put down the conch; but the sudden motion towards it of most of the older boys changed his mind. He tucked the shell under his arm, and crouched back on a rock.

'Then when you get here you build a bonfire that isn't no use. Now you been and set the whole island on fire. Won't we look funny if the whole island burns up? Cooked fruit, that's what we'll have to eat, and roast pork. And that's nothing to laugh at! You said Ralph was chief and you don't give him time to think. Then when he says something you rush off, like, like –'

He paused for breath, and the fire growled at them.

'And that's not all. Them kids. The little 'uns. Who took any notice of 'em? Who knows how many we got?'

Ralph took a sudden step forward.

'I told you to. I told you to get a list of names!'

'How could I,' cried Piggy indignantly, 'all by myself? They waited for two minutes, then they fell in the sea; they went into the forest; they just scattered everywhere. How was I to know which was which?'

Ralph licked pale lips.

'Then you don't know how many of us there ought to be?'

'How could I with them little 'uns running round like insects? Then when you three came back, as soon as you said make a fire, they all ran away, and I never had a chance –'

'That's enough!' said Ralph sharply, and snatched back the conch. 'If you didn't you didn't.'

'–then you come up here an' pinch my specs–'

Jack turned on him.

'You shut up!'

'–and them little 'uns was wandering about down there where the fire is. How d'you know they aren't still there?'

Piggy stood up and pointed to the smoke and flames. A murmur rose among the boys and died away. Something strange was happening to Piggy, for he was gasping for breath.

'That little 'un–' gasped Piggy, 'him with the mark on his face, I don't see him. Where is he now?'

The crowd was as silent as death.

'Him that talked about the snakes. He was down there–'

A tree exploded in the fire like a bomb. Tall swathes of creepers rose for a moment into view, agonized, and went down again. The little boys screamed at them.

'Snakes! Snakes! Look at the snakes!'

In the west and unheeded, the sun lay only an inch or two above the sea. Their faces were lit redly from beneath. Piggy fell against a rock and clutched it with both hands.

'That little 'un that had a mark on his–face–where is–he now? I tell you I don't see him.'

The boys looked at each other fearfully, unbelieving.

'–where is he now?'

Ralph muttered the reply as if in shame.

'Perhaps he went back to the, the–'

Beneath them, on the unfriendly side of the mountain, the drum-roll continued.

Why is this incident important to the novel as a whole?

Write about:

- the words and actions of the characters
- how details of the incident suggest later developments.

---

3 What is the importance of Piggy in *Lord of the Flies*?

---

4 How does Golding explore the theme of power in *Lord of the Flies*?

Write about:

- the struggle between Ralph and Jack
- the role of Piggy
- the actions of Roger.

I'm the King of the Castle

1 Can you sympathise in any way with Hooper? Refer to specific details from the novel to support your ideas.

2 Compare the characters of Kingshaw and Hooper. Refer to specific details from the novel to support your ideas.

3 The following passage is taken from near the beginning of Chapter 12 when Kingshaw and Hooper have been taken on a trip to Leydell Castle.

'What are you going to do?

Kingshaw looked down at him coldly.

'Climb,' he said.

They were inside the ruin. The outer walls reached up very high, and there were odd bits of stone staircase, ending abruptly, so that you could step off into air, or on to parapets, and the remains of pillars, flat-topped like stepping stones. The surface was the colour of damp sand, rough and grainy to the touch, except where bits of moss and lichen grew out of the cracks.

'I bet you won't dare go up far.'

Kingshaw smiled to himself. He moved steadily from stone to stone, along the edge of one wall. He wanted to get as high as he could, up beside the tower.

Hooper watched him from below.

'*You'll* fall off.'

Kingshaw ignored him. He was sure-footed and unhurried, not afraid of any height. He looked down. Hooper was immediately below him. Kingshaw waved an arm.

'Why don't you come up as well?'

His voice echoed round the castle walls. Hooper had got his penknife out and was digging his initials into a slab of stone.

'You'll catch it if anyone sees you. You're not supposed to do that. They can put you in prison for doing it.'

Hooper went on scratching.

The walls were narrower here. Kingshaw went down on all fours, and made sure of the surface with his hands, as he went along, moving very slowly forwards. They had put new mortar between the spaces, though, so that there were no loose stones.

Now the wall went up about a foot, on to the next level. He manoeuvred the step, and then stood upright, carefully, and looked around. Outside the castle, he could see the flat grass and the lake, and his mother and Mr Hooper, sitting on their bench at the far side. He felt high above them, very tall and strong, and safe, too, nobody could touch him. He thought, *this* is all right, I don't care about any of them here, they can't do anything at all to me, I don't care, I don't care. He felt light-headed, exulting in the freedom of it. If he reached his arm up, he might touch the sky.

But even up here, it was warm and airless.

He shouted down to Hooper, 'I'm a bowman, I'm the head warrior of this castle. If I shoot an arrow, I can kill you.'

Hooper looked up.

'I'm the King of the Castle!' Kingshaw began to wave his arms about, and to prance a little, delicately, on top of the wall. If he walked forwards a few yards farther, he would come to a gap. If he could jump it, he would be out on the parapet, leading to the tower.

How does Hill present the episode at Leydell Castle?

What is the importance of this episode to the novel as a whole?

4 The following passage is taken from near the beginning of Chapter 2 where Hooper meets Kingshaw for the first time.

Hooper said, 'Why have you come here?' facing him across the room. Kingshaw flushed brick red. He stood his ground, not speaking. There was a small round table between them. His trunk and a suitcase stood on the floor. 'Why did you have to find somewhere new to live?'

Silence. Hooper thought, now I see why it is better to have a house like Warings, I see why my father goes about clutching the big bunch of keys. We live here, it is ours, we belong. Kingshaw has nowhere.

He walked round the table, towards the window. Kingshaw stepped back as he came.

'Scaredy!'

'No.'

'When my father dies,' Hooper said, 'this house will belong to me, I shall be master. It'll all be mine.'

'That's nothing. It's only an old house.'

Hooper remembered bitterly the land that his grandfather had been forced to sell off. He said quietly, 'Downstairs is something very valuable. Something you've never seen.'

'What then?'

Hooper smiled, looking away out of the window, choosing not to tell. And he was uncertain how impressive the moth collection might really be.

'My grandfather died in this room. Not very long ago, either. He lay and died in that bed. Now it's your bed.' This was not true.

Kingshaw went to the suitcase and squatted down.

'Where did you live before?'

'In a flat.'

'Where?'

'London.'

'Your *own* flat?'

'Yes – no. Well, it was in somebody's house.'

'You were only *tenants*, then.'

'Yes.'

'It wasn't really yours.'

'No.'

'Why didn't your father buy you a proper house?'

Kingshaw stood up. 'My father's dead.' He was angry, not hurt. He wanted to put his fists up to Hooper, and dared not.

Hooper raised his eyebrows. He had learned to do it from a master at school. It seemed an impressive way of looking.

How does Hill present Hooper in this passage? What is the importance of Hooper in the novel as a whole?

5 Remind yourself of the first part of Chapter 10 where Helena Kingshaw speaks to Kingshaw about the incident in Hang Wood.

What does Helena Kingshaw's attitude towards her son here tell you about her?

Write about:

- what is shown about her attitude to Kingshaw, Hooper and Mr Hooper
- how this section prepares the reader for what comes later
- Hill's use of dialogue.

A Kestrel for a Knave

1 The following passage is taken from Billy's interview with the Youth Employment Advisor.

'Now then, Casper, what kind of job had you in mind?'

He shunted the record cards to one side, and replaced them with a blank form, lined and sectioned for the relevant information. CASPER, WILLIAM, in red on the top line. He copied age, address and other details from the record card, then changed pens and looked up.

'Well?'

'I don't know, I haven't thought about it right.'

'Well you should be thinking about it. You want to start off on the right foot don't you?'

'I suppose so.'

'You haven't looked round for anything yet then?'

'No, not yet.'

'Well what would you like to do? What are you good at?'

He consulted Billy's record card again.

'Offices held...Aptitudes and Abilities...right then...would you like to work in an office? Or would you prefer manual work?'

'What's that, manual work?'

'It means working with your hands, for example, building, farming, engineering. Jobs like that, as opposed to pen pushing jobs.'

'I'd be all right working in an office, wouldn't I? I've a job to read and write.'

The Employment Officer printed MANUAL on the form, then raised his pen hand as though he was going to print it again on the top of his head. He scratched it instead, and the nails left white scratches on the skin. He smoothed his fingers carefully across the plot of hair, then looked up. Billy was staring straight past him out of the window.

'Have you thought about entering a trade as an apprentice? You know, as an electrician, or a bricklayer or something like that. Of course the money isn't too good while you're serving your apprenticeship. You may find that lads of your own age who take dead end jobs will be earning far more than you; but in those jobs there's no satisfaction or security, and if you do stick it out you'll find it well worth your while. And whatever happens, at least you'll always have a trade at your finger tips won't you?...

'Well, what do you think about it? And as you've already said you feel better working with your hands, perhaps this would be your best bet. Of course this would mean attending Technical College and studying for various examinations, but nowadays most employers encourage their lads to take advantage of these facilities, and allow them time off to attend, usually one day a week. On the other hand, if your firm wouldn't allow you time off in the day, and you were still keen to study, then you'd have to attend classes in your own time. Some lads do it. Some do it for years, two and three nights a week from leaving school, right up to their middle twenties, when some of them take their Higher National, and even degrees.

'But you've got to if you want to get on in life. And they'll all tell you that it's worth it in the end…Had you considered continuing your education in any form after leaving?…I say, are you listening, lad?'

'Yes.'

'You don't look as though you are to me. I haven't got all day you know, I've other lads to see before four o'clock.'

He looked down at Billy's form again.

'Now then, where were we? O, yes. Well if nothing I've mentioned already appeals to you, and if you can stand a hard day's graft, and you don't mind getting dirty, then there are good opportunities in mining…'

'I'm not goin' down t'pit.'

'Conditions have improved tremendously…'

'I wouldn't be seen dead down t'pit.'

'Well what do you want to do then? There doesn't seem to be a job in England to suit you.'

What attitude does the Employment Officer present towards Billy in the passage?

What do you think the novel has to say about the opportunities available to Billy?

---

2 Remind yourself of the section of the novel where Mr Farthing goes to visit Billy and watches him fly Kes.

How does Hines present Mr Farthing here and elsewhere in the novel? What is his importance to the novel as a whole?

---

3 How do you respond to Hines's presentation of Jud?

Write about:

- Jud's relationship with Billy
- his attitude towards other characters
- his importance in the novel as a whole.

---

4 What kind of picture does Hines create of school life in this novel?

Write about:

- the attitude of the Headteacher, Mr Gryce
- the attitude of other teachers
- Billy's feelings about school.

---

5 Why is Kes so important to Billy? How does Hines create a sense of Billy's feelings towards the bird?

Of Mice and Men

1 The following passage is taken from the beginning of the novel where Steinbeck describes the opening scene.

> A few miles south of Soledad, the Salinas River drops in close to the hill-side bank and runs deep and green. The water is warm too, for it has slipped twinkling over the yellow sands in the sunlight before reaching the narrow pool. On one side of the river the golden foothill slopes curve up to the strong and rocky Gabilan mountains, but on the valley side the water is lined with trees – willows fresh and green with every spring, carrying in their lower leaf junctures the debris of the winter's flooding; and sycamores with mottled, white, recumbent limbs and branches that arch over the pool. On the sandy bank under the trees the leaves lie deep and so crisp that a lizard makes a great skittering if he runs among them. Rabbits come out of the brush to sit on the sand in the evening, and the damp flats are covered with the night tracks of 'coons, and with the spread pads of dogs from the ranches, and with the split-wedge tracks of deer that come to drink in the dark.
>
> There is a path through the willows and among the sycamores, a path beaten hard by boys coming down from the ranches to swim in the deep pool, and beaten hard by tramps who come wearily down from the highway in the evening to jungle-up near water. In front of the low horizontal limb of a giant sycamore there is an ash-pile made by many fires; the limb is worn smooth by men who have sat on it.

How does Steinbeck create a sense of atmosphere, both here and elsewhere in the novel?

2 How does Steinbeck explore the theme of loneliness in the novel?

Write about:

- why some characters may feel lonely
- how language contributes to a sense of the characters' loneliness
- how the settings or circumstances contribute to a sense of loneliness.

3 Remind yourself of the part of the novel where Curley attacks Lennie. What do Curley's actions here, and elsewhere in the novel, reveal about his character?

Write about:

- how Curley treats his wife
- how other characters respond to him
- his actions at the end of the novel.

4 The relationship between George and Lennie is at the centre of the novel. How does Steinbeck present the relationship?

Write about:

- how Lennie relies on George
- why George looks after Lennie
- the description of the two characters
- the ending of the novel.

To Kill a Mockingbird

1 What is Jem's function and importance in the novel?

2 The following passage is taken from near the beginning of Chapter 1 and describes Dill.

Dill was from Meridian, Mississippi, was spending the summer with his aunt, Miss Rachel, and would be spending every summer in Maycomb from now on. His family was from Maycomb County originally, his mother worked for a photographer in Meridian, had entered his picture in a Beautiful Child contest and won five dollars. She gave the money to Dill, who went to the picture show twenty times on it.

'Don't have any picture shows here, except Jesus ones in the court-house sometimes,' said Jem. 'Ever see anything good?'

Dill had seen *Dracula*, a revelation that moved Jem to eye him with the beginning of respect. 'Tell it to us,' he said.

Dill was a curiosity. He wore blue linen shorts that buttoned to his shirt, his hair was snow white and stuck to his head like duck-fluff; he was a year my senior but I towered over him. As he told us the old tale his blue eyes would lighten and darken; his laugh was sudden and happy; he habitually pulled at a cowlick in the centre of his forehead.

When Dill reduced Dracula to dust, and Jem said the show sounded better than the book, I asked Dill where his father was: 'You ain't said anything about him.'

'I haven't got one.'

'Is he dead?'

'No...'

'Then if he's not dead you've got one, haven't you?'

Dill blushed and Jem told me to hush, a sure sign that Dill had been studied and found acceptable. Thereafter the summer passed in routine contentment. Routine contentment was: improving our treehouse that rested between giant twin chinaberry trees in the backyard, fussing, running through our list of dramas based on the works of Oliver Optic, Victor Appleton and Edgar Rice Burroughs. In this matter we were lucky to have Dill. He played the character parts formerly thrust upon me – the ape in *Tarzan*, Mr Crabtree in *The Rover Boys*, Mr Damon in *Tom Swift*. Thus we came to know Dill as a pocket Merlin, whose head teemed with eccentric plans, strange longings, and quaint fancies.

How does Harper Lee present Dill in this passage?

What is the importance of Dill in the novel as a whole?

3 How does Harper Lee present Scout's development through a series of learning experiences in this novel?

4 What is the function of Boo Radley in the novel?

5 How does the trial of Tom Robinson explore the idea of prejudice in the novel?

EXAMINER'S TIP

Literary texts can be open to more than one interpretation and questions do not necessarily have 'right' or 'wrong' answers. They do want you to explore your ideas though and support those ideas with references to the texts. The points given here are suggested ideas you might explore but do not present the only ideas that you might include in an answer.

Lord of the Flies

❶ Here are some ideas that you should cover in your answer.

Ralph

- He tries to organise things – it is his idea to elect a chief.
- He is calm.
- Many of the others look up to him because of his size and attractive appearance.
- He is fair – he wants to involve Jack even though Jack has not been elected chief.
- He is able to command silence from the group, which shows his leadership qualities.

Jack

- He is arrogant.
- He automatically thinks he should be chief.
- He feels angry and humiliated when he is not voted chief.
- He likes to get his own way.

This passage prepares us for what is to come later in the novel because:

- it gives us ideas on the personalities of Jack and Ralph
- it sows the seeds of the conflict that develops between them.

EXAMINER'S TIP

When writing about characters think about:
- *what they do*
- *what they say*
- *what others say about them*
- *their relationship with other characters*
- *the ways in which the writer uses language to describe and present them.*

❷ Here are some ideas.
- It shows the disorganised state of the boys.
- Piggy has sensible things to say.
- Jack's dislike of Piggy is obvious.
- They realise that some of the *'little 'uns'* have died in the fire.

- This introduces the idea of boys being killed, which escalates as the novel goes on.
- It intensifies the developing sense of conflict between the boys.

❸ Here are some ideas.
- Piggy is a friend to Ralph.
- He supports Ralph throughout.
- He is the most intelligent of the boys.
- He puts forward practical ideas.
- Jack dislikes him and this creates a sense of conflict.
- The others make fun of him because he is physically unfit, wears glasses etc.
- This makes him an easy target for Jack.
- He is killed at the end when Roger rolls a huge boulder onto him. This marks a turning point as it is the first deliberate killing.

❹ Here are some ideas.
- Ralph has power because he is voted chief but Jack wants power.
- The power struggle develops around Jack's arrogant and vicious nature against Ralph's fair-minded attitude.
- Piggy comes between them – Ralph, being fair, tries to protect him against Jack's attack.
- Roger becomes Jack's henchman and his sadistic nature brings about the death of Piggy.
- From this point, the conflict between Ralph and Jack becomes a life or death one for Ralph.

EXAMINER'S TIP

Remember to support your ideas with detailed references to the text.

I'm the King of the Castle

❶ Here are some ideas.
- Hooper's mother died when he was four and so he has been deprived of a mother's love.
- He was sent away to a boarding school at an early age.
- He doesn't have a close relationship with his father.
- He has not had many 'normal' childhood experiences.
- He does not seem to have many friends.

EXAMINER'S TIP

Gather as much evidence from the text as you can to support the views you put forward.

② Here are some ideas.
- Kingshaw and Hooper have a number of features in common.
- Both are lonely and have few friends.
- Both have lost one parent.
- Neither relates to the adults in their lives.
- Both reveal the need for adult affection and comfort when they are upset.
- Both are isolated and withdraw into their own worlds.
- Both have intense fears.
- They have differences too, though.
- Hooper is aggressive whereas Kingshaw does not appear naturally aggressive.
- Hooper exploits Kingshaw's fears.
- Hooper appears cold and resentful.

EXAMINER'S TIP

When writing about a character, remember they are not real people, they are creations of the writer. Focus on how writers use language to create impressions of their characters.

③ Here are some ideas.
- The incident on the day trip out is presented as a further step in the conflict between Hooper and Kingshaw.
- For once, Kingshaw has found something at which he can be the dominant one – climbing.
- Briefly, Kingshaw gains a psychological advantage over Hooper.
- This advantage is short-lived, though, and the reader's hope that Kingshaw might, at last, be breaking free of Hooper's intimidation is soon dashed.

④ Here are some ideas.
- Hooper makes it clear that he is resentful of Kingshaw's arrival.
- He emphasises the fact that it is his house and Kingshaw does not belong there.
- He tries his best to make Kingshaw feel uncomfortable.
- He is important to the scheme of the novel because it is his conflict with, and persecution of, Kingshaw that is at the heart of the novel.

⑤ Here are some ideas.
- Helena Kingshaw does not understand her son or appreciate how he feels.
- She is more concerned that they fit in with Mr Hooper's ideas.
- She hopes that a relationship will develop between her and Mr Hooper.
- She feels very dependent on Mr Hooper and sees him as a man who provides security for herself and her son.
- She agrees with everything he says and does everything she can to gain his favour and win acceptance.

A Kestrel for a Knave

① Here are some ideas.
- The Employment Officer seems to lack both interest in and understanding of Billy.
- He fails totally to give any helpful advice to Billy.
- He seems sharp and abrupt.
- He doesn't understand the kind of person Billy is.
- He shows little interest in finding out what Billy is good at or interested in.
- This section shows us the kind of future that awaits Billy.
- His only realistic option seems to go down the pit.
- No one is going to help Billy.

② Here are some ideas.
- Mr Farthing shows a genuine, kind interest in Billy.
- He is the only one in the book who seems to be on Billy's side and wants to help him.
- He is shown to be a good teacher who interests the class.
- He is good at getting Billy to talk about Kes.
- He treats Billy as an equal and does not speak down to him.

③ Here are some ideas.
- Jud and Billy are half-brothers.
- Jud bullies Billy and constantly mocks him.
- He regards himself as a tough man and expects others to recognise that.
- He does not have a close relationship with his mother.
- He is important in the novel because he represents an unfeeling, brutal character who kills Kes in the end.
- He shows us the kind of life that might await Billy.

EXAMINER'S TIP

Remember that personal responses should be supported by clear and appropriate references to the text.

④ Here are some ideas.
- School life for Billy is presented as a miserable and pointless experience.
- Gryce is a tyrant and a bully who shows no understanding of the young people in his charge.
- Violence is the norm in school, from both teachers and other pupils.
- Crossley is unsympathetic with no sense of humour or feeling for his job.
- Sugden is sarcastic, cruel and self-centred.
- Billy hates school and sees it as a waste of time because it has nothing at all to offer him.

5 Here are some ideas.
- Kes offers Billy an escape into another world.
- Billy loves animals and nature and Kes provides him with a kind of friendship.
- He loves the bird.
- Training her has encouraged him to read and learn about hawks.
- She has enabled him to develop his skills in handling and training her.
- She provides him with enjoyment in an otherwise miserable life.
- Billy is trapped in his life but through flying Kes he can experience a kind of freedom.

Of Mice and Men

1 Here are some ideas.
- The description of springtime creates a sense of freshness and hope.
- New leaves are growing and the wildlife is active.
- There is a sense of peace and harmony in the natural setting.
- Imagery is used to create the sense of atmosphere.
- Visual description creates a sense of mood and setting.
- You should select some specific examples of your choice to illustrate this point.

2 Here are some ideas.
- Although their lives might be lonely, George and Lennie have each other.
- Loneliness is explored through Crookes – a victim of racial prejudice.
- Candy deals with his loneliness by gossiping.
- Curley's wife also shows a kind of loneliness through her isolation.
- George often plays solitaire – a game for one.

3 Here are some ideas.
- Curley is a vicious bully and a coward.
- He neglects his wife.
- No one likes him and other characters see him as aggressive, jealous and mean-minded.

EXAMINER'S TIP

Make sure that you do not re-tell the story in your answer. You should analyse the texts, not simply describe them.

4 Here are some ideas.
- Lennie is very childlike and relies on George to tell him what to do and generally look after him.
- George has taken responsibility for Lennie for several reasons.
- He possibly feels sorry for him.
- He likes Lennie.

- Lennie provides him with companionship.
- George is the opposite of Lennie – he is quick-witted and intelligent whereas Lennie is very big and strong but mentally like a small child.
- George recognises that Lennie helps him in terms of companionship but can also be a nuisance.
- In the end, he kills Lennie out of compassion.

To Kill a Mockingbird

1 Here are some ideas.
- Jem is Scout's older brother and is seen as her protector as well as her companion.
- He seeks to imitate his father and becomes very conscious of human rights.
- We see him maturing through Scout's eyes.
- Throughout the novel, he is always aware of his responsibility to his younger sister.
- Jem functions as a contrast to Scout.
- After the trial, he is puzzled and bewildered by the workings of the adult world and feels a strong sense of injustice.
- It is his sense of fair play and justice that makes him want to be a lawyer like his father.

2 Here are some ideas.
- Dill is a great storyteller and tells Jem about his life, often exaggerating the details.
- When his mother remarries, he feels neglected – he introduces himself to Scout and Jem by saying 'I'm little, but I'm old'.
- Dill's position as a child contrasts to Scout's childhood and shows that Scout is lucky to have people like her father and Calpurnia to look after her.
- Dill also has things in common with Boo Radley – he has an unhappy home life and is very sensitive to the harshness of the outside world.
- Unlike Boo, who retreats from the world into his dark house, Dill escapes into his fantasy world.

EXAMINER'S TIP

Make sure that you focus closely on the ways in which language is used to create a sense of place, character, experience or atmosphere. Use specific examples to illustrate your ideas.

3 Here are some ideas.
- Scout is the narrator of the story and all the experiences are seen through her eyes.
- Throughout the novel, the events and situations that she sees around her contribute to her growth and development.
- She sympathises with Mayella Ewell at the trial, sensing Mayella's loneliness.

- Her imagination has been developed through reading.
- She is open-minded and accepts people for who they are, not making any social distinction about Calpernia's Negro Church, for example.
- Initially she accepts people like the Cunninghams and the Ewells as equals but, as the novel develops, she learns that sometimes it is necessary to make distinctions between people.
- Through the events of the novel, she also learns about the complex white social relationships and the prejudices harboured by some white people for black people.

④ Here are some ideas.
- Boo is one of the dominant characters in the novel, even though he never really appears as an individual.
- He creates a sense of mystery in the first part of the novel, often being talked and joked about by the children.
- They first regard him as some sort of monster, but gradually learn that he is a gentle person.
- In the end, he saves their lives by killing Bob Ewell in order to protect them.
- He presents a symbol of kindness in the novel, leaving gifts for Scout and Jem in the tree.
- In the end, he is a symbol of bravery and compassion.

⑤ Here are some ideas.
- It is clear from the outset that things are stacked against Tom in the trial.
- The trial reveals the great discrepancy between the laws governing the white people and the laws governing the black people.
- A white woman cannot be accused of lying, particularly when it is her word against that of a negro.
- The general opinion is that it is better to condemn a negro than face the truth – that a white woman made sexual advances to him.
- Tom becomes the victim of white prejudice, even though Atticus proves beyond doubt that Tom could not possibly have committed the crime.
- Innocently convicted, he desperately tries to escape and is tragically killed, therefore emphasising the ultimate injustice.

EXAMINER'S TIP

Always make sure that you plan how you are going to answer a question before you begin to write.

Post-1914 prose texts

CHAPTER 3

Pre-1914 poetry

See also Chapter 10 in Letts *Revise GCSE English and English Literature.*

Try this sample GCSE question and then compare your answer with the Grade C and Grade A model answers on pages 41 to 43.

AQA Anthology – Specification B *Best Words*

Spend about 40 minutes on this.

Leave enough time to read through and correct what you have written.

Look again at *My Last Duchess* by Robert Browning. Compare this poem with one other from the Pre-1914 selection that presents a very different relationship between two people.

These two answers are at grades C and A. Compare them with your answer and think about how you might have improved your own response.

GRADE C ANSWER

Layla

Indicates focus on questions.

I am going to compare 'My Last Duchess' by Robert Browning with 'Shall I compare thee' by William Shakspear. Both these poems present a certan kind of relationship between two people. ✓

Sound ideas supported by appropriate quotation.

In 'My Last Duchess' a duke is talking to someone about his wife who is now dead and showing him a picture of her on the wall. It sounds as if the picture is very lifelike because it says 'Looking as if she were alive'. ✓ At first the Duke seems to admire the portrate and the beauty of his dead Duchess:

'The depth and passion of that earnest glance.'

Aware of the Duke's attitude to the Duchess and good focus on the language of the poem. Good use of supporting quotation.

But then the Duke seems to not like how the Duchess was when she was alive. ✓ In a way he seems jealous when he says ''twas not / Her husband's presence only, called that spot / Of joy into the Duchess' cheek.' ✓ He says that everyone liked his wife and that she liked everyone. He seems jellous of this and that she thanked

Again good awareness shown here.

people for small things ✓ as if these things were as important as the family name that he had given her by marrying her:

Appropriate supporting quotation.

'She thanked men, – good! but thanked
Somehow – I know not how – as if she ranked
My gift of a nine-hundred-years-old name
With everybody's gift.' ✓

Personal response based on textual evidence. Goes on to explore the personal response with good focus on the text.

He sounds as if he was really possesive of her but that in the end he had her killed because she could not be his alone: ✓ 'I gave commands / Then all smiles stopped'. This makes me think that he killed her in some way. Maybe he had her poisioned but he doesn't seem worried about telling someone else about it. It does show him to be cold and heartless and he did not care about his wife. He just wanted to keep her to himself like a possesion. ✓

Comparison being made.

This is quite different ✓ to the kind of relationship that is shown in 'Shall I compare thee…' In this poem Shakespeare seems to express real love for the other person. In the poem he praises the beauty of the other person as being better than a Summer's day –

'Shall I compare thee to a Summer's day?
Thou art more lovely and more temperate.'

Sound comment based on text.

He obviously feels really emotionally inspired by the person and feels that their beauty will last forever: ✓
'But thy eternall Sommer shall not fade,
Nor loose possession of that faire thou ow'st.' ✓

Comparative point made.

He means that even though time passed her beauty will live on forever in the lines of this poem. This seems an expression of real love, not like the possessive love in 'My Last Duchess'. ✓

Show more detailed focus on 'My Last Duchess' – needs to develop ideas more fully on 'Shall I compare thee'.

15/25

SPELLCHECK!

Shakespeare	jealous
certain	poisoned
portrait	possession

Grade booster ····⟩ move C to B
- Need to develop ideas on both poems fully.
- Technical accuracy needs attention.

GRADE A ANSWER

Mina

Focus on question.

The two poems 'My Last Duchess' by Robert Browning and 'First Love' by John Clare present relationships, ✓ although the sentiments expressed within them are very different.

Sets the context here.

In 'My Last Duchess' we read of a Duke who is introducing the portrait ✓ of his late wife, his 'Last Duchess' to an onlooker. The Duke is seen to express a disturbingly cold attitude to his late wife and this creates a somewhat sinister feel to the poem. ✓ For example, the opening of the poem where the Duke states: 'That's my last Duchess painted on the wall' ✓ is coldly factual and suggests that she was merely an object that he possessed. It is the portrait of the Duchess and not her that the Duke calls 'a wonder' ✓ and although he does not state how they met, we know that the artist was chosen 'by design'. The feelings expressed by John Clare for his love are markedly different. ✓ For example, a much more emotional, loving feel is evident as the poem expresses the depth of feeling: '... ne'er was struck before that hour with love so sudden and so sweet'.

Aware of the Duke's feelings coming through – good analytical comment.

Close focus on vocabulary with illustrative examples.

Comparison being made – aware of the contrasting effects achieved.

Analysis of structure and comment on effects.

Comparative points on structure and effects of the structure.

'First Love' is written in three stanzas, which trace the development of the poet's love, and the rhyme scheme creates a sense of unity between the stanzas. There appears to be a formal structure ✓ to the content of the poem, and the poem seems to be a collection of outpourings expressed by a lover in emotional distress. In contrast, ✓ 'My Last Duchess' is a single-stanza poem written in rhyming couplets but, because of the content of the poem, and the mid-line breaks in the rhythm, no sense of harmony is evident – this complements the sentiments expressed in the poem. ✓ Perhaps this contrast is best seen in the final rhyming couplet of the poem compared to Clare's emotional statement: 'My heart has left its dwelling place / And can return no more'. ✓ Although the exact

Close analytical focus on the ending of the poems supported by appropriate quotation.

Very perceptive analysis.

meaning of the last sentiment is ambiguous, it clearly focuses on feelings of the heart. However, 'My Last Duchess' concludes: 'Taming a sea-horse, thought a rarity, / Which Claus of Innsbruck cast in bronze for me'. This final sentiment is one focussing on possession, materialism and conquest. ✓

Further detailed analysis of 'My Last Duchess'. Less detailed comments on 'First Love' but a good conclusion to the essay.

One aspect of relationships that differs greatly in the two poems is that of unconditional love. ✓ The line in 'My Last Duchess': 'Somehow – I know not how – as if she ranked / My gift of a nine-hundred-years-old name / With anybody's gift.' suggests that the Duke wanted gratitude, something in return for the material benefits he had to offer, some sort of recognition of him being the best. ✓ The Duke's self-centredness, his conditional approach to relationships is, however, a one way expectation as we see in his line: 'I choose / Never to stoop'. The Duke's arrogance ✓ and lack of personal insight into his own failings contrasts greatly with the pain expressed by Clare in 'First Love'.

22/25

Grade booster ⤍ move A to A*
More detailed analysis of 'First Love' needed so that both poems are given equal treatment.

QUESTION BANK

Spend about 45 minutes on each question in this section. Each question carries **25 marks**.

AQA Anthology – Specification A

1 In *The Laboratory* by Robert Browning, the poet creates an underlying sense of menace. Compare this poem with one poem by Simon Armitage, one poem by Carol Ann Duffy and one other poem from the Pre-1914 selection in which the poets create a sense of danger or menace.

2 Compare how poets use form, structure and language in at least four of the poems you have studied. Write about *Inversnaid* by Gerard Manley Hopkins and compare it with one poem by Simon Armitage, one poem by Carol Ann Duffy and one other poem from the Pre-1914 Bank.

3 Compare four or more poems from the selection, which you have found interesting because of the ways in which the poets use imagery. Write about *Patrolling Barnegat* and compare it with one poem by Simon Armitage, one poem by Carol Ann Duffy and one other poem from the Pre-1914 Bank.

4 a) Compare how love is presented in *On My First Sonne* by Ben Jonson and *Catrin* by Gillian Clarke.
   b) Compare these poems with two more poems, one by Seamus Heaney and one from the Pre-1914 Poetry Bank.

5 Compare how bitterness or resentment against other people is shown in *My Last Duchess* and three other poems – one other Pre-1914 poem, one poem by Carol Ann Duffy and one by Simon Armitage.

6 a) Compare how Clare writes about nature in *Sonnet* with Heaney's presentation of it in *Storm on the Island*.
   b) Compare these poems with two more poems, one by Carol Ann Duffy and one from the Pre-1914 Poetry Bank.

7 In *The Laboratory*, Browning uses the first-person narrative to create his effects. Compare the ways in which this poem is written with *The Field-Mouse* by Gillian Clarke, one poem by Simon Armitage and one other poem from the Pre-1914 Poetry Bank.

8 Compare Hardy's presentation of death in *The Man He Killed* with Heaney's presentation of it in *Mid-Term Break*. Compare these poems with one by Gillian Clarke and one other from the Pre-1914 Poetry Bank.

AQA Anthology – Specification B *Best Words*

1 Look again at *To Autumn* by John Keats. Compare this poem with one other from the Pre-1914 selection that uses vivid description and imagery. You should look closely at the language used.

2 Read again *Porphyria's Lover* by Robert Browning. Compare this poem with one other from the Pre-1914 selection that presents love in a very different way. You should look closely at the language used.

3 Read again *To His Coy Mistress* by Andrew Marvell. Compare this poem with one other from the Pre-1914 selection in which the poetic voice creates a strong impression.

4 Look again at *Ballad*. Compare this poem with one other from the Pre-1914 selection in which the poet uses poetry to tell a story.

5 Read again *To a Mouse* by Robert Burns. Compare this poem with one other from the Pre-1914 selection that describes aspects of nature.

Songs of Innocence and Experience – Blake

1 Explore the ways in which the poems in *Songs of innocence and Experience* convey Blake's views on religion. You should base your answers on two poems of your choice from the selection.

2 What views of childhood does Blake express in *Songs of Innocence and Experience*? You should base your answer on two poems from the selection.

3 Compare the ways in which Blake expresses his ideas in *The Lamb* with one other poem of your choice from the selection.

4 Compare the ways in which Blake uses symbolism to express his ideas in *The Sick Rose* and *The Divine Image*.

5 How do the poems in *Songs of Innocence and Experience* explore two different views of the world? You should base your answers on two poems of your choice from the selection.

War Poems ed. Martin

1 Compare the ways in which Southey and Tennyson create an impression of war in *The Battle of Blenheim* and *The Charge of the Light Brigade*.

2 Explore the attitudes expressed towards war by Hardy in *Drummer Hodge* and Kipling in *The Hyaenas*.

3 Compare Hardy's *A Wife in London* with one other poem from the Pre-1914 selection that explores the effects of war on an individual.

4 Examine the ways in which Whitman creates his effects in *Come up from the Fields Father*. Compare this poem with one other from the Pre-1914 selection that you have found particularly effective.

5 Compare the ways in which poets use particular incidents or events to express their attitudes towards war. You should base your answer on two poems from the Pre-1914 selection.

A Choice of Poets ed. Edward or Hewett (depending on edition)

1 Compare the views put forward by Wordsworth in *The World is Too Much With Us* with the ideas put forward by Blake in a poem of your own choosing.

2 Choose one poem by Wordsworth and one poem by Blake and compare the ways in which they use language to convey their ideas and achieve their effects.

3 Explore Blake's view of London as expressed in his poem *London*. Compare this poem with one by Wordsworth in which he describes an urban environment.

4 Compare the ways in which Wordsworth and Blake use nature or description of nature in their poems.

5 Compare Wordsworth's *To a Skylark* with Blake's *The Tiger*. Explore how each poet uses language to achieve his effects.

Selected Poems of Hardy

1 Read these two poems carefully.

Neutral Tones

We stood by a pond that winter day,
And the sun was white, as though chidden of God,
And a few leaves lay on the starving sod;
    —They had fallen from an ash, and were gray.

Your eyes on me were as eyes that rove
Over tedious riddles of years ago;
And some words played between us to and fro
    On which lost the more by our love.

The smile on your mouth was the deadest thing
Alive enough to have strength to die;
And a grin of bitterness swept thereby
    Like an ominous bird a-wing…

Since then, keen lessons that love deceives,
And wrings with wrong, have shaped to me
Your face, and the God-curst sun, and a tree
    And a pond edged with grayish leaves.

In Tenebris

'Percussus sum sicut foenum, et aruit cor meum.' – *Ps.* ci.

    Wintertime nighs;
But my bereavement-pain
It cannot bring again:
    Twice no one dies

    Flower-petals flee;
But, since it once hath been,
No more that severing scene
    Can harrow me.

    Birds faint in dread:
I shall not lose old strength
In the lone frost's black length:
    Strength long since fled!

    Leaves freeze to dun;
But friends can not turn cold
This season as of old
    For him with none.

    Tempests may scath;
But love can not make smart
Again this year his heart
    Who no heart hath.

    Black is night's cope;
But death will not appal
One who, past doubtings all,
    Waits in unhope.

With careful reference to the language Hardy uses, explore the ways these two poems create a sense of bitterness or despair.

2 Explore Hardy's view of war as presented in two of the following poems:

* *Drummer Hodge*
* *A Wife in London*
* *On the Departure Platform*
* *The Man He Killed*

3 Read the following two poems carefully.

To Lizbie Browne

I

Dear Lizbie Browne,
Where are you now?
In sun, in rain? –
Or is your brow
Past joy, past pain,
Dear Lizbie Browne?

II

Sweet Lizbie Browne,
How you could smile,
How you could sing!–
How archly wile
In glance-giving,
Sweet Lizbie Browne!

III

And, Lizbie Browne,
Who else had hair
Bay-red as yours,
Or flesh so fair
Bred out of doors,
Sweet Lizbie Browne?

IV

When, Lizbie Browne,
You had just begun
To be endeared
By stealth to one,
You disappeared,
My Lizbie Browne!

ANSWERS ON PAGE 51 ANSWERS ON PAGE 51 ANSWERS ON PAGE 51 ANSWERS ON PAGE 51

V

Ay, Lizbie Browne,
So swift your life,
And mine so slow,
You were a wife
Ere I could show
Love, Lizbie Browne.

VI

Still, Lizbie Browne,
You won, they said,
The best of men
When you were wed…
Where went you then,
O Lizbie Browne?

VII

Dear Lizbie Browne
I should have thought,
'Girls ripen fast.'
And coaxed and caught
You ere you passed,
Dear Lizbie Browne!

VIII

But, Lizbie Browne,
I let you slip;
Shaped not a sign;
Touched never your lip
With lip of mine,
Lost Lizbie Browne!

IX

So, Lizbie Browne,
When on a day
Men speak of me
As not, you'll say,
'And who was he?' —
Yes, Lizbie Browne!

The Ruined Maid

'O 'Melia, my dear, this does everything crown!
Who could have supposed I should meet you in Town?
And whence such fair garments, such prosperi-ty?' –
'O didn't you know I'd been ruined?' said she.

–'You left us in tatters, without shoes or socks,
Tired of digging potatoes, and spudding up docks;
And now you've gay bracelets and bright feathers three!' –
'Yes: that's how we dress when we're ruined,' said she.

–'At home in the barton you said "thee" and "thou",
And "thik oon", and "theäs oon", and "t'other"; but now
Your talking quite fits 'ee for high compa-ny!' –
'Some polish is gained with one's ruin,' said she.

–'Your hands were like paws then, your face blue and bleak
But now I'm bewitched by your delicate cheek,
And your little gloves fit as on any la-dy!' –
'We never do work when we're ruined,' said she.

–'You used to call home-life a hog-ridden dream,
And you'd sigh, and you'd sock; but at present you seem
To know not of megrims or melancho–ly!' –
'True. One's pretty lively when ruined,' said she.

–'I wish I had feathers, a fine sweeping gown,
And a delicate face, and could strut about Town!' –
'My dear – a raw country girl, such as you be,
Cannot quite expect that. You ain't ruined,' said she.

Explore the ways in which Hardy uses language in these poems to tell a story.

 Look again at *The Darkling Thrush* and *I Look into my Glass*. With careful reference to the language of each poem, explore how Hardy presents his ideas.

QUESTION BANK ANSWERS

EXAMINER'S TIP

Poems can be open to many different interpretations and so these kinds of questions do not have 'right' or 'wrong' answers but they do want you to explore your own ideas on the poems. The suggestions given here are simply an indication of some of the things you might write about and are not the only things you could put in an answer.

AQA Anthology – Specification A

1 Here are some ideas.
- Look carefully at the language that Browning uses to create an underlying sense of menace.
- Examine the poet's use of imagery and its effects.
- Choose your comparison poems carefully, making sure that, in them, the poets create a sense of danger or menace.

2 Here are some ideas.
- Look carefully at how Manley uses language, form and structure in his poem *Inversnaid*.
- Examine the poet's use of imagery and its effects.
- Choose your comparison poems carefully, making sure that you note how language, form and structure are used by the poets to create their desired effects.

3 Here are some ideas.
- Look carefully at how Whitman uses imagery in his poem *Patrolling Barnegat*.
- Examine the poet's use of imagery and its effects.
- Choose your comparison poems carefully, making sure you note how imagery is used by the poets to create their desired effects.

4 Here are some ideas.
- Look carefully at how Jonson presents love in *On My First Sonne* and Clarke presents it in *Catrin*.
- Examine the poets' use of imagery and its effects.
- Choose your comparison poems carefully, making sure you note how imagery is used by the poets to create their desired effects.

5 Here are some ideas.
- Look carefully at how Browning presents bitterness and resentment against other people in *My Last Duchess*.
- Examine the poet's use of imagery and its effects.

- Choose your comparison poems carefully, making sure that bitterness and resentment against other people are expressed by the poets.

6 Here are some ideas.
- Look carefully at the language that Clare uses to describe nature and compare it with Heaney's use of language in *Storm on the Island*.
- Examine the poets' use of imagery and its effects.
- Choose your comparison poems carefully, making sure you have enough to say about them.

7 Here are some ideas.
- Look carefully at how Browning uses the first-person narrative and compare the effects created here with those in *The Field-Mouse*.
- Examine the poets' use of imagery and its effects.
- Choose your comparison poems carefully, making sure you note how narrative voices are used by the poets to create their desired effects.

8 Here are some ideas.
- Look carefully at how Hardy presents death in *The Man He Killed* and Heaney's presentation of it in *Mid-Term Break*.
- Examine the poet's use of imagery and its effects.
- Choose your comparison poems carefully, making sure you note how imagery is used by the poets to create their desired effects.

AQA Anthology – Specification B *Best Words*

1 Here are some ideas.
- Your answer should focus on the way Keats expresses his ideas.
- Imagery is particularly important in this poem.
- Look closely at the language of the poem.
- Choose carefully the poem you compare with this, picking one that contains some vivid description.
- Compare the ways each poet uses language.

2 Here are some ideas.
- Your answer should focus on Browning's presentation of love in this poem.
- Look closely at the effects created by the poem.
- Choose carefully the poem you compare with this, picking one that presents love in some way.
- Compare the ways each poet uses language.

❸ Here are some ideas.
  • Your answer should focus on the way Marvell expresses his ideas.
  • Look at the persuasive techniques Marvell uses.
  • Look closely at the language of the poem.
  • Choose carefully the poem you compare with this, picking one that has created a strong impression.
  • Compare the ways each poet uses language.

❹ Here are some ideas.
  • Your answer should focus on the ways in which *Ballad* tells a story.
  • Look closely at the language and structure of the poem.
  • Choose carefully the poem you compare with this, picking one that also tells a story of some kind.
  • Compare the ways each poem tells its story.

❺ Here are some ideas.
  • Your answer should focus on the way Burns expresses his ideas on nature.
  • Look closely at the language and imagery of the poem.
  • Choose carefully the poem you compare with this, picking one that describes some aspect of nature.
  • Compare the ways each poet uses language.

Songs of Innocence and Experience

❶ Here are some ideas.
  • Your answer should focus on what the poems reveal to you about Blake's views on religion.
  • Imagery is particularly important in your chosen poems.
  • Look closely at the language of the poems.
  • Choose the poems carefully, making sure you can write about how they show Blake's views on religion.

❷ Here are some ideas.
  • Your answer should focus on what the poems reveal to you about Blake's views on childhood.
  • Imagery and symbolism are likely to be important in your chosen poems.
  • Look closely at the language of the poems.
  • Choose the poems carefully, making sure you can write about how they show Blake's views on childhood.

❸ Here are some ideas.
  • Your answer should focus on how Blake expresses his ideas in *The Lamb* and another poem of your choice.
  • Imagery and symbolism may be important in your chosen poems.
  • Look closely at the language of the poems.

• Choose your comparison poem carefully, making sure you have plenty of ideas to write about.

❹ Here are some ideas.
  • Your answer should focus closely on Blake's use of symbolism in *The Sick Rose* and *The Divine Image*.
  • Comment on the effects created by this use of symbolism.
  • Look closely at the language of the poems.

❺ Here are some ideas.
  • Your answer should focus on what the poems reveal to you about Blake's views of the world.
  • Imagery is likely to be particularly important in your chosen poems.
  • Look closely at the language of the poems.
  • Choose the poems carefully, making sure you can write about how they show Blake's views.

EXAMINER'S TIP

When answering a question on poetry:
  • *read the poems through very carefully several times and form some ideas on them*
  • *write in well-structured sentences and check that your spelling and punctuation are accurate*
  • *focus directly on the question.*

War Poems

❶ Here are some ideas.
  • Your answer should focus on the impressions of war created in the poems.
  • Look carefully at the imagery of the poems and the ways in which the poets use language, structure and rhythm to create their effects.
  • Identify specific features from the poems, comment on them and analyse their effects.

❷ Here are some ideas.
  • Your answer should focus on *Drummer Hodge* and *The Hyaenas* and the attitudes to war that the poets express in them.
  • Look carefully at the imagery of the poems and the ways in which the poets use language, structure and rhythm to create their effects.
  • Look also at the use of setting and atmosphere here.
  • Identify specific features from the poems, comment on them and analyse their effects.

❸ Here are some ideas.
  • The central focus of your answer should be on *A Wife in London* and another poem of your choice.

- Look carefully at the imagery of the poems and the ways in which the poets use language, structure and rhythm to create their effects.
- Identify specific features from the poems, comment on them and analyse their effects.
- Choose your comparison poem carefully, making sure you have ideas about it.

EXAMINER'S TIP

If you are asked to compare poems, make sure you include some comparative points, rather than simply writing about one poem and then about the other.

4 Here are some ideas.
- The central focus of your answer should be on *Come up from the Fields Father* and another poem of your choice.
- Look carefully at the imagery of the poems and the ways in which the poets use language, structure and rhythm to create their effects
- Identify specific features from the poems, comment on them and analyse their effects.
- Choose your comparison poem carefully, making sure you have ideas about it.

5 Here are some ideas.
- This question gives you a free choice of poems so make sure you select your poems carefully – you need to select poems in which the poets use particular event or incidents to express their attitudes towards war.
- Look carefully at the imagery of the poems and the ways in which the poets use language, structure and rhythm to create their effects.
- Identify specific features from the poems, comment on them and analyse their effects.

EXAMINER'S TIP

Remember to focus on specific details of the ways in which poets use language. Comment on the effectiveness of devices that might be used, such as metaphor, simile, alliteration etc. Don't just identify them but explain the effects they create within the poem.

A Choice of Poets
1 Here are some ideas.
- The central focus of your answer should be on *The World is Too Much With Us* and a poem by Blake of your choice.
- Look carefully at the imagery of the poems and the ways in which the poets use language, structure and rhythm to create their effects.

- Identify specific features from the poems, comment on them and analyse their effects.
- Choose your comparison poem carefully, making sure you have ideas about it.

2 Here are some ideas.
- This question gives you a free choice of poems, one by Wordsworth and one by Blake, so make sure you select your poems carefully – you need to select poems that you feel you can write about.
- Look carefully at the imagery of the poems and the ways in which the poets use language, structure and rhythm to create their effects.
- Identify specific features from the poems, comment on them and analyse their effects.

3 Here are some ideas.
- The central focus of your answer should be on *London* by Blake and a poem by Wordsworth of your choice.
- The poem you choose should describe or comment on an urban environment in some way.
- Look carefully at the imagery of the poems and the ways in which the poets use language, structure and rhythm to create their effects.
- Identify specific features from the poems, comment on them and analyse their effects.
- Choose your comparison poem carefully, making sure you have ideas about it.

4 Here are some ideas.
- This question gives you a free choice of poems, one by Wordsworth and one by Blake.
- The focus is on the ways in which the poets use nature or descriptions of nature in their poems.
- Choose your poems carefully – you need to select poems that you feel you can write about.
- Look carefully at the imagery of the poems and the ways in which the poets use language, structure and rhythm to create their effects.
- Identify specific features from the poems, comment on them and analyse their effects.

5 Here are some ideas.
- The central focus of your answer should be on *The Skylark* by Wordsworth and *The Tiger* by Blake.
- Look carefully at the imagery of the poems and the ways in which the poets use language, structure and rhythm to create their effects.
- Identify specific features from the poems, comment on them and analyse their effects.
- Choose your comparison poem carefully, making sure you have ideas about it.

EXAMINER'S TIP

The rhyme scheme and rhythm patterns of a poem might play an important part in the overall effect of the poem. Remember, though, that it is not enough just to describe the rhyme scheme or rhythm pattern – you need to explain the effects that they create.

Selected Poems of Hardy

1 Here are some ideas.
- The central focus of your answer should be on the poems given.
- Both poems possess a tone of great bitterness or despair.
- Look carefully at the imagery of the poems and the ways in which Hardy uses language, structure and rhythm to create his effects.
- Identify specific features from the poems, comment on them and analyse their effects.

2 Here are some ideas.
- This question gives you a choice of poems, all of which express a view of war.
- Choose your poems carefully – you need to select poems that you feel you can write about.
- Look carefully at the imagery of the poems and the ways in which Hardy uses language, structure and rhythm to create his effects.
- Identify specific features from the poems, comment on them and analyse their effects.

3 Here are some ideas.
- The central focus of your answer should be on the poems given.
- Both poems tell a story and you should focus on the techniques Hardy uses to tell each tale.
- Look carefully at the imagery of the poems and the ways in which the poet uses language, structure and rhythm to create his effects.
- Identify specific features from the poems, comment on them and analyse their effects.

4 Here are some ideas.
- The central focus of your answer should be on *The Darkling Thrush* and *I Look into My Glass*.
- Look carefully at the imagery of the poems and the ways in which Hardy uses language, structure and rhythm to create his effects.
- Identify specific features from the poems, comment on them and analyse their effects.
- Make sure you compare the poems.

FOR MORE INFORMATION ... SEE REVISE GCSE ENGLISH AND ENGLISH LITERATURE ... CHAPTER 10

CHAPTER 4

Post-1914 poetry

See also Chapter 10 in Letts *Revise GCSE English and English Literature.*

Try this sample GCSE question and then compare your answer with the Grade C and Grade A model answers on pages 56 to 58.

AQA Anthology – Specification A

Spend about 40 minutes on this.

Leave enough time to read through and correct what you have written.

Compare the ways in which the poets express their ideas about the relationship between parent and child. Write about *Follower* by Seamus Heaney and compare it with one poem by Gillian Clarke and two poems from the Pre-1914 Poetry Bank.

These two answers are at grades C and A. Compare them with your answer and think about how you might have improved your own response.

GRADE C ANSWER

Clear focus and supporting quotations.

Identifies a key point here.

A valid comparison.

Could be expressed more effectively but a valid idea supported by relevant quotation.

Good comparative point made here.

A relevant comparison.

A fourth poem introduced. Some good ideas but not fully developed.

Frank

In 'Follower' Heaney writes about a memory from when he was little. He remembers following his father when his father was ploughing. You can tell that he looked up to his father because he calls him 'An expert' and that he was able to plough 'the furrow exactly'. ✓ He also remembers how he used to sometimes stumble when he followed his father and how sometimes his father would carry him on his back. This also shows how strong the father was compared to the child. Now, though, the child has become a man and the father has grown old. It is now the father who follows the son and sometimes stumbles. Even so there is a strong sense of a bond between father and son.

Another poem which examines the relationship between parent is 'Catrin' by Gillian Clarke. This poem, though, ✓ contains much more of the idea of conflict as well as love. Even from birth Clarke says:

'I can remember you, our first
Fierce confrontation.'

This idea of love and argueing is a common one between mother and daughter who both want to have their own lives. ✓ Clarke writes about their:

'struggle to become
Separate. We want, we shouted,
To be two, to be ourselves.' ✓

This is different to the way Heaney feels. He seems to like the idea of being linked to his father. Even so I think that Clarke's poem shows that she loves her daughter even though they fight.

In Blake's 'The Little Boy Lost and the Little Boy Found', the father seems to adopt a cold hearted atittude towards the son and desserts him. ✓ This is different to the Heaney and Clarke poems where there is a strong feeling of love between parent and child (despite the fights in 'Catrin'). ✓ Another poem where there is a strong sense of love between parent and child is 'On My First Sonne'. ✓ This is different, though, because the child has died. The poet is very upset about this and at first blames himself, thinking that he was too sinful to have a child. He then comforts himself with thinking about how his son has avoided all the pain and suffering of life. What comes out of the poem is the strong sense of love that the poet had for his son. I think this sense of love is also present in 'Follower' and even 'Catrin' but in 'The Little Boy Lost and the Little Boy Found' the love comes from God and not the parent. ✓

14/25

Grade booster ···} move C to B

- Need to develop ideas on poems more fully.
- Ideas need to be expressed more effectively.

GRADE A ANSWER

Louis

Clearly aware of Heaney's admiration for his father.

In this poem Heaney writes about a childhood memory of how he used to follow his father's footsteps ✓ as he ploughed the fields on their farm. He admires his father's skill in ploughing and the way in which he handles the team of horses pulling the plough. However, Heaney uses this memory to explore a deeper idea ✓ – that of how now his father is old and he is grown up their roles have become reversed. When he was a child he wanted to be like his father who appeared powerful and strong but following him the child:

Sees a deeper significance in Heaney's development of his idea.

Appropriate quotation.

'Fell sometimes on the polished sod;
Sometimes he rode me on his back.'

A perceptive point fluently made.

This conveys to the reader just how close the relationship was between father and son ✓ but it also shows how following him was not always easy on the rough ground. Now he is grown up though it is his father who is the follower and he now keeps stumbling:

Appropriate supporting quotation.

'...But today
It is my father who keeps stumbling
Behind me...' ✓

Even so the bond between them is still there and '...will not go away'.

Good comparative point and sound analysis of Clarke's ideas. Good supporting quotation.

Similarly 'Catrin' by Gillian Clarke explores the relationship between parent and child, this time mother and daughter. ✓ I think this poem explores a typical mother/daughter relationship which consists of both love and conflict. This contrast is emphasised through the imagery that Clarke uses:

'the tight
red rope of love which we both
fought over' ✓

Good comparison of the poets' use of imagery in their poems. Some perceptive analysis here.

This use of imagery compares ✓ with Heaney's use of imagery to describe his father in 'Follower' with:

'His shoulder globed like a full sail strung
Between the shafts and the furrow.'

Clarke's metaphor uses the idea of the umbilical chord still attached to the mother and the child both of them struggling to be separate. Heaney's simile ✓ uses the idea of a sail filled with the wind to suggest a sense of power.

Aware of differences too.

The poems differ ✓ though in that in 'Catrin' mother and daughter want to be separated to have their own identities whereas in 'Follower' Heaney is happy that he and his father are forever linked.

Ideas not fully developed on this poem.

'On My First Sonne' is another poem that explores the relationship between parent and child. This time the poet is writing about the death of his son. The poet feels that it is his own sins that have caused him to lose his son: ✓
'My Sinne has too much hope of thee, lov'd boy'
He then goes on, though, to comfort himself that his son has escaped the pains of life and of growing old.

Again, ideas not fully developed on this poem.

Blake's 'Little Boy Lost and Little Boy Found' is also about a father and a son relationship. In this poem there is a sense of suffering created because he is deserted by his father and so becomes lost. The repetition of speech creates a sense of the boy's anxiety at becoming lost: ✓

'Speak father, speak to your little boy
Or else I should be lost.'

Like 'On My First Sonne' this poem contains a religious element as the little boy is saved by God. All these poems, then, explore some aspect of the relationship between parent and child but look at it from different viewpoints and in different ways.

21/25

Grade booster ⋯⋅⟩ move A to A*
More development needed of ideas and comparisons of the two Pre-1914 poems.

Spend about 45 minutes on each question in this section. Each question carries **25 marks**.

AQA Anthology – Specification A

1 In *Hitcher*, Simon Armitage adopts the 'voice' of a character to express the ideas of the poem. Compare this poem with one poem by Carol Ann Duffy and two poems from the Pre-1914 Poetry Bank, where poets write from the point of view of particular characters.

Remember to compare:

- the 'voice' or character 'speaking'
- how the poets create a sense of this 'voice'
- how you respond to the poems.

2 Compare the ways in which the poets use imagery to create effects in four poems that you have studied. Write about *Kid* by Simon Armitage and compare it with at least one poem by Carol Ann Duffy and two poems from the Pre-1914 Poetry Bank.

Remember to compare:

- the different images the poets use
- the effects created by the imagery.

3 Compare the ways in which the poets write about memories of the past in their poems. Beginning with *Death of a Naturalist* by Seamus Heaney, compare at least four poems you have studied, including at least one poem by Gillian Clarke and two poems from the Pre-1914 Poetry Bank.

Write about:

- the ideas the poems contain
- how they use memories about the past
- similarities and differences between the poems
- how you respond to the poems.

4 In *Cold Knap Lake*, Gillian Clarke writes of a childhood memory about an apparently drowned girl being pulled from a lake. Compare this poem with at least three others from the selection in which the poets write about moving experiences. Include one poem by Seamus Heaney and two poems from the Pre-1914 Poetry Bank.

Remember to compare:

- the experiences the poets write about
- how they write about themes
- how you respond to the poems.

AQA Anthology – Specification B *Best Words*

1 Look again at *An Advancement of Learning* by Seamus Heaney. Compare it with one other poem of your choice from the Post-1914 selection in which the poet vividly describes an event or a memory.

2 Look again at *A Martian Sends a Postcard Home* by Craig Raine. Compare it with one other poem from the Post-1914 selection in which the poet describes something in an unusual way.

3 In *Long Distance* by Tony Harrison, he explores how he comes to terms with death in his family. Compare the poem with one other from the Post-1914 selection in which the poet writes about coming to terms with an emotional experience.

4 Look again at *Once Upon a Time* by Gabriel Okara in which he describes the learning experiences of growing up from childhood to adulthood. Compare it with one other poem from the selection in which the poet writes about a learning experience.

5 In her poem *Blackberrying*, Sylvia Plath uses a variety of imagery to achieve her effects. Compare this poem with one other poem in the Post-1914 selection in which the poet uses imagery to create effects.

Edexcel Anthology

1 *Identity*
Re-read the poem *Follower* by Seamus Heaney in which the poet describes the relationship between father and son. Compare this poem with AT LEAST ONE other poem from *Identity* in which the poet writes about the relationship between parent and child.

2 *Nature*
Re-read *Wind* by Ted Hughes and choose ONE other poem from *Nature* in which the poet writes about a particular aspect of nature. Compare the ways the writer or writers present their subjects.

3 *Nature*
Re-read *Trout* by Seamus Heaney and choose ONE other poem from *Nature* that describes a living creature.
Compare the ways in which the writers create a strong impression of their subjects.

Axed Between the Ears ed. Kitchen

1 Look again at *Travelling through the Dark* by William Stafford. Compare this poem with one other from the selection that also deals with the death of an animal. You should refer closely to the poets' use of language.

2 Look again at the poem *Green Beret* by Ho Thien, which describes an incident in the Vietnam War. Compare the poem with one other from the selection that also deals with conflict of some kind. You should refer closely to the ways in which the poets' use language.

3 Look again at *Old Age Report* by Adrian Mitchell. Compare the poem with one other from the selection that also deals with old age. You should refer closely to the poets' use of language.

War Poems ed. Martin

1 Look again at *Who's for the Game* by Jessie Pope. Compare this poem with one other from the selection that expresses a different view of war. You should refer closely to the ways in which the poets use language to achieve their effects.

2 Look again at *Vergissmeinnicht* by Keith Douglas. Compare the poem with one other from the selection that expresses the tragic waste of war. You should refer closely to the poets' use of language.

3 Look again at *Dulce Et Decorum Est* by Wilfred Owen. Compare the poem with one other from the selection in which the poet uses vivid imagery to express the horror of war. You should refer closely to the poet's or poets' use of language.

A Choice of Poets ed. Edward or Hewett (depending on edition)

1 Read again *The Evacuee* in which Thomas describes a young child evacuated during the Second World War. Compare this poem with one other from the selection in which the poet describes a person. You should refer closely to the ways in which the poet or poets use language.

2 Look again at *The Silken Tent* by Robert Frost. Compare this poem with one other from the selection in which the poet or poets use language to create effects.

3 Read again *A Blackbird Singing* by R. S. Thomas. Compare this poem with one other from the selection that describes an aspect of nature. You should refer closely to the ways in which the poet or poets use language.

ANSWERS ON PAGE 62 ANSWERS ON PAGE 62 ANSWERS ON PAGE 62 ANSWERS ON PAGE 62

EXAMINER'S TIP

▶▶▶ *Poems can be open to many different interpretations and so these kinds of questions do not have 'right' or 'wrong' answers but they do want you to explore your own ideas on the poems. The suggestions given here are just an indication of some of the things you might write about and are not the only things that you could put in an answer.*

AQA Anthology – Specification A

❶ Here are some ideas.
- The voice of the speaker is weary, tired and disillusioned.
- The 'matter of fact' tone is used to give a sense of the voice.
- Look at the language the speaker uses.
- You need to select carefully the other poems from the anthology that you will compare with *Hitcher*.
- Make sure that those you choose are ones where the poets write from the point of view of characters.

❷ Here are some ideas.
- Look at the images of childhood the poet uses.
- Explore how the language of the comic book interlinks with the images Armitage uses.
- You need to select carefully the other poems you choose to write about.
- Make sure they use imagery in some way.

❸ Here are some ideas.
- In *Death of a Naturalist,* Heaney recounts a vivid childhood memory.
- He uses this memory to explore the idea of growing up and learning about himself.
- Select the other poems you write about carefully, making sure that you have plenty to say about them.

❹ Here are some ideas.
- Look at Clarke's use of the first-person to write the poem.
- Explore the atmosphere she creates in the poem.
- Examine the images she uses.
- Select the other poems you write about carefully, making sure that in these poems the poets write about moving experiences.

EXAMINER'S TIP

▶▶▶ *When answering a question on poetry:*
- *read the poems through very carefully several times and form some ideas on them*
- *write in well-structured sentences and check that your spelling and punctuation are accurate*
- *focus directly on the question.*

AQA Anthology – Specification B Best Words

❶ Here are some ideas.
- Heaney recounts a particular memory from his past.
- This memory presented a learning experience for him.
- Choose the poem that you compare with this one carefully, making sure that it describes an event or memory.

❷ Here are some ideas.
- Examine the unusual method that Raine uses in this poem.
- He imagines how we might appear to a Martian visiting Earth.
- The poem is rather like a series of crossword clues for you to solve.
- Choose the poem you compare with this one carefully, focusing on an unusual way of presenting ideas.

❸ Here are some ideas.
- Your answer should focus on the way Harrison expresses his ideas and emotions.
- Look closely at the language of the poem.
- Choose the poem you compare with this one carefully, picking one in which the poet writes about an emotional experience.

❹ Here are some ideas.
- Okara writes about the loss of traditional African culture.
- Note the idea of the fear of losing something valuable.
- Choose your poem for comparison carefully, making sure that, in it, the poet writes about some kind of learning experience.

❺ Here are some ideas.
- Plath uses a number of images in her poem.
- Look carefully at them, making sure you explain the effects she creates through them.
- Make sure the poem you choose for comparison makes use of imagery.
- Do not simply describe the images; explain the effects that the poets create by using them.

EXAMINER'S TIP

Remember to focus on specific details of the ways in which poets use language. Comment on the effectiveness of devices that might be used, such as metaphor, simile, alliteration etc. Don't just identify them but explain the effects they create within the poem.

Edexcel Anthology

❶ Here are some ideas.
- The poem is based on a memory of Heaney's father ploughing.
- It shows the closeness of the father/son relationship.
- Make sure you choose carefully the poem or poems you are to compare with *Follower*. Your comparison poem(s) should deal with the relationship between parent and child.

❷ Here are some ideas.
- Look carefully at the language and imagery that Hughes uses.
- Explore the effects that he achieves through this use of language.
- Choose your comparison poem carefully, focusing on the ways in which the subjects are presented.

❸ Here are some ideas.
- Look carefully at the language Heaney uses to describe the trout.
- Examine the poet's use of imagery and its effects.
- Choose your comparison poem carefully, making sure it describes a living creature.

Axed Between the Ears

❶ Here are some ideas.
- Look carefully at the language that Stafford uses to describe the death of an animal.
- Examine the poet's use of imagery and its effects.
- Choose your comparison poem carefully, making sure it describes the death of an animal.

❷ Here are some ideas.
- Look carefully at the language that Ho Thien uses to deal with conflict of some kind.
- Examine the poet's use of imagery and its effects.
- Choose your comparison poem carefully, making sure it describes dealing with some sort of conflict.

❸ Here are some ideas.
- Look carefully at the language that Mitchell uses to deal with old age.
- Examine the poet's use of imagery and its effects.
- Choose your comparison poem carefully, making sure it deals with old age.

War Poems

❶ Here are some ideas.
- Look carefully at the language Pope uses to express a different view of war.
- Examine the poet's use of imagery and its effects.
- Choose your comparison poem carefully, making sure it expresses a view of war.

❷ Here are some ideas.
- Look carefully at the language Douglas uses to express the tragic waste of war.
- Examine the poet's use of imagery and its effects.
- Choose your comparison poem carefully, making sure it describes the waste of war.

❸ Here are some ideas.
- Look carefully at how Owen uses vivid imagery to express the horror of war.
- Examine the poet's use of imagery and its effects.
- Choose your comparison poem carefully, making sure it describes the horror of war.

EXAMINER'S TIP

Think about the ways in which all the elements of a poem work together to create the overall effect.

A Choice of Poets

❶ Here are some ideas.
- Look carefully at the language Thomas uses to describe a person.
- Examine the poet's use of imagery and its effects.
- Choose your comparison poem carefully, making sure it describes a person.

❷ Here are some ideas.
- Look carefully at the language Frost uses to create effects.
- Examine the poet's use of imagery and its effects.
- Choose your comparison poem carefully, making sure it uses language to create effects.

❸ Here are some ideas.
- Look carefully at the language Thomas uses to describe an aspect of nature.
- Examine the poet's use of imagery and its effects.
- Choose your comparison poem carefully, making sure it describes an aspect of nature.

EXAMINER'S TIP

The rhyme scheme and rhythm patterns of a poem might play an important part in the overall effect of the poem. Remember, though, that it is not enough just to describe the rhyme scheme or rhythm pattern – you need to explain the effects that they create.

CHAPTER 5

Pre-1914 drama

See also Chapters 7 and 8 in Letts *Revise GCSE English and English Literature.*

Try this sample GCSE question and then compare your answer with the Grade C and Grade A model answers on pages 65 to 67.

Spend about 40 minutes on this.

Leave enough time to read through and correct what you have written.

Examine the importance of Friar Lawrence in *Romeo and Juliet*.

These two answers are at grades C and A. Compare them with your answer and think about how you might have improved your own response.

GRADE C ANSWER

Opens with a focus on the question.

Adopts a structured approach.

Use of appropriate quotation here.

Sound points but not always well expressed.

A second idea developed.

Again, the expression here could be improved.

Some relevant ideas but not always clearly expressed. Tends to lack more detailed development.

SPELLCHECK!

tragedy
tragic
Shakespeare

James

Friar Lawrence has a very important role to perform in the action of the play. ✓ The play is a tragedy and, as such, the ending of the play must be a tragic one. Shakespeare uses the character of Friar Lawrence to create the tragic ending he wanted.

He contributes to the tragedy in a number of ways. Firstly he agrees to marry Romeo and Juliet secretly: ✓

'Come, come with me, and we will make short work;
For, by your leave, you shall not stay alone
Till Holy Church incorporate two in one.' ✓

Although he means well by marrying them it is because no one else knows about the marriage that Juliet is in trouble later. ✓ This happens when her parents arrange for her to marry Paris. She knows she can't do this because she is already married but the trouble is no one else knows.

However, through the creation of this situation Shakespeare can then bring into play the device of the potion which makes Juliet look as though she is dead. This is Friar Lawrence's idea and it is the taking of this potion which leads directly to them all being dead at the end. The role of the Friar Lawrence, therefore, is essential in creating the emding of the play.

Another factor involving Friar Lawrence which helps to create tragedy is the letter that he writes to Romeo. The letter not getting to him again contributes to the tragedy because Romeo thinks that Juliet is really dead.

If Friar Lawrence had managed to get to the Capulet vault before Romeo and let him know what was going on it ✓ would have been alright. Of course, Shakespear needs the Friar to turn up late so that Romeo thinks that Juliet is really dead. In this way Friar Lawrence is also vital to the way the plot works out.

He also tells everyone else about what has happened when the Prince and all the others arrive. ✓ He tells them of everything which as well as informing the other characters of events also serves as a summary for the audience of the whole plot. This helps to draw the drama to a conclusion.

14/25

Grade booster ┈┈> move C to B
- Ideas need developing in greater depth.
- Expression needs improvement.
- Technical accuracy needs attention.

These two answers are at grades C and A. Compare them with your answer and think about how you might have improved your own response.

GRADE A ANSWER

Cassie

Focused opening.

Although in some ways one of the more minor characters in the play in terms of how frequently he appears on stage, Friar Lawrence has an important role to play in the development of the plot. ✓ It is clear that he is respected and trusted by all in the play but ultimately it is he who is indirectly responsible for the tragic outcome of the action.

We first hear mention of Friar Lawrence at the end of Act II, Scene ii after Romeo and Juliet have met and fallen in love. As Romeo leaves Juliet he says:

> 'Hence will I to my ghostly father's cell,
> His help to crave, and my dear hap to tell.' ✓

A relevant idea.

It is significant here that the first person that Romeo intends to turn to for advice concerning his love for a Capulet, is Friar Lawrence. ✓

Tends to be adopting a narrative approach here.

At the beginning of the next scene we see Friar Lawrence for the first time as he enters, collecting herbs. Romeo enters and the Friar immediately detects that Romeo has been out all night. On hearing of Romeo's love for Juliet he offers his wise advice on love but when he realises the strength of Romeo's feelings he accepts the situation. However, he does have another motive for his rapid acceptance as he immediately sees the love of the two young people as a possible means of bringing to an end the feud between the Montagues and the Capulets: ✓

Begins to analyse the Friar's motivation – supported by a relevant quotation.

> '...I'll thy assistant be;
> For this alliance may so happy prove,
> To turn your household's rancour to pure love.' ✓

In the hope of achieving this end he agrees to marry the young couple.

A little later the Friar offers more advice to Romeo when he tries to persuade him to be patient as they await the arrival of Juliet. His words here, though, also carry a prophetic warning that ironically foretells what is to happen later: ✓

Perceptive point here backed up with very appropriate quotation.

> 'These violent delights have violent ends,
> And in their triumph die, like fire, and powder,
> Which as they kiss consume.' ✓

Relevant discussion of the friar's actions.

A little later, when Romeo has killed Tybalt the Friar's advice to Romeo is also important. ✓ It is he who calms Romeo's wild talk after the Prince has imposed banishment on him. He points out to him all the reasons he has to be grateful and eventually he succeeds in calming him down. He immediately takes control and arranges for Romeo to go to Mantua until the Friar can sort the situation out.

Begins to develop another idea here.

As well as being a friend and advisor to Romeo he is also a friend and advisor to Juliet. He is the Friar she gives her confession to and, in fact, ✓ this provides the reason she visits the Friar's cell when he marries the couple. When her parents arrange for her to marry Paris she is completely desperate and the Friar is the only one she can turn to. It is at this point in the plot that the fateful plan to use the sleeping potion on Juliet is conceived. However, it is worth noting that this is presented as a desperate situation and Juliet is threatening to kill herself rather than be married to Paris. In this sense, though,

Evaluating the importance of Friar Lawrence.

Friar Lawrence is the most important character ✓ in the development of the incidents which build up to the final tragedy. In this way then Shakespeare uses the character as a key element and a way of setting in action the means by which he can bring about the tragic ending of the play.

Effectively summarises the key ideas.

His advice to the lovers, then, is vital to the plot. His agreeing to marry Romeo and Juliet sets up the problems which are developed later in the plot. ✓ The idea of the potion is his and Shakespeare uses this plan to move the plot towards the final tragedy. As a part of this it is Friar Lawrence who instructs Friar John to deliver the message to Romeo in Mantua but fatefully the message is not delivered. Finally, his failure to arrive at the tomb when Romeo arrives is also essential to the plot and the creation of the tragic ending.

22/25

Grade booster ⋯⟩ move A to A*

- Broader interpretation of the role of friar Lawrence is needed.
- Requires a little more detail in the analysis.

Spend about 45 minutes on each question in this section. Each question carries **25 marks**.

***Much Ado About Nothing* – Shakespeare**

1 Write about the different views of love that are presented in the play.

2 Remind yourself of Act 1, Scene iii where Don John reveals his true nature. What do you think about the presentation of this character? Do you feel that his presence poses a threat to the comic tone of the play?

3 Read the following extract carefully. It is from Act 1 Scene i.

'DON PEDRO, CLAUDIO, BENEDICK, BALTHAZAR and DON JOHN the Bastard' enter the orchard

DON PEDRO:	Good Signior Leonato, are you come to meet your trouble? The fashion of the word is to avoid cost, and you encounter it.
LEONATO:	Never came trouble to my house in the likeness of your grace. For trouble being gone, comfort should remain: but when you depart from me, sorrow abides and happiness takes his leave.
DON PEDRO:	You embrace your charge too willingly. I think this is your daughter.
LEONATO:	Her mother hath many times told me so.
BENEDICK:	Were you in doubt, sir, that you asked her?
LEONATO:	Signior Benedick, no – for then were you a child.
DON PEDRO:	You have it in full, Benedick – we may guess by this what you are, being a man. Truly the lady fathers herself. Be happy, lady, for you are like an honourable father. [*He talks apart with Hero and Leonato*]
BENEDICK:	If Signior Leonato be her father, she would not have his head on her shoulders for all Messina, as like him as she is.
BEATRICE:	I wonder that you will still be talking, Signior Benedick – nobody marks you.
BENEDICK:	What, my dear Lady disdain! are you yet living?
BEATRICE:	It is possible disdain should die, while she hath such meet food to feed it as Signior Benedick? Courtesy itself must convert to disdain, if you come in her presence.
BENEDICK:	Then is courtesy a turn-coat. But it is certain I am loved of all ladies, only you excepted: and I would I could find in my heart that I had not a hard heart, for truly I love none.
BEATRICE:	A dear happiness to women – they would else have been troubled with a pernicious suitor. I thank God and my cold blood, I am of your humour for that. I had rather hear my dog bark at a cow than a man swear he loves me.
BENEDICK:	God keep your ladyship still in that mind, so some gentleman or other shall 'scape a predestinate scratched face.
BEATRICE:	Scratching could not make it worse, an 'twere such a face as yours were.
BENEDICK:	Well, you are a rare parrot-teacher.
BEATRICE:	A bird of my tongue is better than a beast of yours.
BENEDICK:	I would my horse had the speed of your tongue, and so good a continuer. But keep your way a God's name – I have done.
BEATRICE:	You always end with a jade's trick. I know you of old.

What do you learn of Beatrice's attitude to Benedick in this section? How is their relationship central to the play?

4 Read the following passage. It is from Act 4 Scene i.

Before the altar of a church
DON PEDRO, DON JOHN, LEONATO, FRIAR FRANCIS, CLAUDIO,
BENEDICK, HERO, BEATRICE, &c.

LEONATO:	Come Friar Francis, be brief – only to the plain form of Marriage, and you shall recount their particular duties afterwards.
FRIAR:	You come hither, my lord, to marry this lady?
CLAUDIO:	No.
LEONATO:	To be married to her; friar, you come to marry her.
FRIAR:	Lady, you come hither to be married to this Count?
HERO:	I do.
FRIAR:	If either of you know any inward impediment why you should not be conjoined, I charge you on your souls to utter it.
CLAUDIO:	Know you any, Hero?
HERO:	None my lord.
FRIAR:	Know you any, Count?
LEONATO:	I dare make his answer, 'none.'
CLAUDIO:	O, what men dare do! What men may do! What men daily do, not knowing what they do!
BENEDICK:	How now! Interjections? Why then, some be of laughing, as 'ah! ha! he!'
CLAUDIO:	Stand thee by, Friar. Father, by your leave – Will you with free and unconstrained soul Give me this maid your daughter?
LEONATO:	As freely, son, as God did give her me.
CLAUDIO:	And what have I to give you back whose worth May counterpoise this rich and precious gift?
DON PEDRO:	Nothing, unless you render her again.
CLAUDIO:	Sweet prince, you learn me noble thankfulness. There Leonato, take her back again, Give not this rotten orange to your friend, She's but the sign and semblance of her honour. Behold how like a maid she blushes here! O, what authority and show of truth Can cunning sin cover itself withal! Comes not that blood, as modest evidence, To witness simple virtue? Would you not swear, All you that see her, that she were a maid, By these exterior shows? But she is none: She knows the heat of a luxurious bed: Her blush is guiltiness, not modesty.
LEONATO:	What do you mean my lord?
CLAUDIO:	Not to be married, Not to knit my soul to an approved wanton.
LEONATO:	Dear my lord, if you in your own proof, Have vanquished the resistance of her youth, And made defeat of her virginity –

CLAUDIO:	I know what you would say: if I had known her,
	You will say she did embrace me as a husband,
	And so extenuate the 'forehand sin.
	No, Leonato,
	I never tempted her with word too large,
	But as a brother to his sister, showed
	Bashful sincerity, and comely love.
HERO:	And seemed I ever otherwise to you?
CLAUDIO:	Out on thee! Seeming, I will write against it.
	You seem to me as Dian in her orb,
	As chaste as is the bud ere it be blown:
	But you are more intemperate in your blood
	Than Venus, or those pamp'red animals
	That rage in savage sensuality.
HERO:	Is my lord well that he doth speak so wide?
LEONATO:	Sweet prince, why speak not you?
DON PEDRO:	What should I speak?
	I stand dishonoured that have gone about
	To link my dear friend to a common stale.
LEONATO:	Are these things spoken, or do I but dream?
DON JOHN:	Sir, they are spoken, and these things are true.
BENEDICK:	This looks not like a nuptial.
HERO:	True! O God!

How do you respond to the presentation of Claudio both in this scene and elsewhere in the play?

5 How do you respond to the character of Dogberry? What do you feel he and his associates add to the play as a whole?

Romeo and Juliet – Shakespeare

1 In the following extract from Act 3 Scene iii, Friar Lawrence tells Romeo of his banishment.

ROMEO:	Father what news? What is the Prince's doom?
	What sorrow craves acquaintance at my hand,
	That I yet know not.
F.LAWRENCE:	Too familiar
	Is my dear son with such sour company.
	I bring thee tidings of the Prince's doom.
ROMEO:	What less than doomsday is the Prince's doom?
F.LAWRENCE:	A gentler judgement vanished from his lips,
	Not body's death, but body's banishment.
ROMEO:	Ha, banishment? Be merciful, say 'death';
	For exile hath more terror in his look,
	Much more than death. Do not say 'banishment'.
F.LAWRENCE:	Here from Verona art thou banished.
	Be patient, for the world is broad and wide.

ROMEO:	There is not world without Verona walls,
	But purgatory, torture, hell itself.
	Hence banished is banished from the world.
	And world's exile is death. Then 'banished'
	Is death mis-termed. Calling death 'banished',
	Thou cut'st my head off with a golden axe,
	And smilest upon the stroke that murders me.
F.LAWRENCE:	O deadly sin! O rude unthankfulness!
	Thy fault our law calls death, but the kind Prince
	Taking thy part hath rushed aside the law,
	And turned that black word death to banishment.
	This is dear mercy, and thou seest it not.
ROMEO:	'Tis torture and not mercy. Heaven is here
	Where Juliet lives, and every cat and dog,
	And little mouse, every unworthy thing,
	Live here in heaven, and may look on her,
	But Romeo may not. More validity,
	More honourable state, more courtship lives
	In carrion flies than Romeo. They may seize
	On the white wonder of dear Juliet's hand,
	And steal immortal blessing from her lips,
	Who even in pure and vestal modesty
	Still blush, as thinking their own kisses sin.
	But Romeo may not, he is banished.
	Flies may do this, but I from this must fly;
	They are free men, but I am banished.
	And sayest thou yet that exile is not death?
	Hadst thou no poison mixed, no sharp-ground knife,
	No sudden mean of death, though ne'er so mean,
	But 'banished' to kill me? Banished?
	O friar, the damned use that word in hell;
	Howling attends it. How hast thou the heart,
	Being a divine, a ghostly confessor,
	A sin-absolver, and my friend professed,
	To mangle me with that word 'banished'?
F.LAWRENCE:	Thou fond mad man, hear me a little speak.
ROMEO:	O thou wilt speak again of banishment.
F.LAWRENCE:	I'll give thee armour to keep off that word,
	Adversity's sweet milk, philosophy,
	To comfort thee though thou art banished.
ROMEO:	Yet 'banished'? Hang up philosophy,
	Unless philosophy can make a Juliet,
	Displant a town, reverse a prince's doom,
	It helps not, it prevails not. Talk no more.
F.LAWRENCE:	O then I see that madmen have no ears.
ROMEO:	How should they, when that wise men have no eyes?
F.LAWRENCE:	Let me dispute with thee of thy estate.
ROMEO:	Thou canst not speak of that thou dost not feel.
	Wert thou as young as I, Juliet thy love,
	An hour but married, Tybalt murdered,
	Doting like me, and like me banished,
	Then mightst thou speak, then mightst thou tear thy hair,
	And fall upon the ground, as I do now,
	Taking the measure of an unmade grave.

How does Shakespeare present Romeo at this point in the play? How do his words and actions here compare with the ways in which he behaves elsewhere in the play?

 Explore the presentation of Mercutio and his contribution to the overall effect of *Romeo and Juliet*.

3 Remind yourself of the final scene of the play (Act V, Scene iii) from the point where Paris enters at the beginning of the scene to the point where Romeo kills himself. What kind of atmosphere does Shakespeare create here and what effect does it have on the conclusion of the play?

4 Compare the characters of Romeo and Juliet in the play.

5 Examine the roles played by fate and coincidence in *Romeo and Juliet*.

The Merchant of Venice – Shakespeare

1 Explore the main themes of *The Merchant of Venice* and the ways in which Shakespeare presents them.

 How does Shakespeare present the nature of love and friendship in *The Merchant of Venice*?

You should write about:

• Antonio's friendship with Bassanio
• the love of Bassanio and Portia
• any other ideas of your own.

3 Remind yourself of Act III, Scene i, where Shylock voices the suffering of the Jews. How does Shakespeare present the conflict between Christian and Jew in *The Merchant of Venice*?

4 The following passage is taken from the beginning of Act I, Scene iii, where we see Shylock for the first time.

> *Venice*
>
> *Enter* BASSANIO *and* SHYLOCK
>
> | SHYLOCK: | Three thousand ducats-well. |
> |---|---|
> | BASSANIO: | Ay sir, for three months. |
> | SHYLOCK: | For three months-well. |
> | BASSANIO: | For the which as I told you, Antonio shall be bound. |
> | SHYLOCK: | Antonio shall become bound-well. |
> | BASSANIO: | May you stead me? Will you pleasure me? Shall I know your answer? |

SHYLOCK:	Three thousand ducats for three months, and Antonio bound.
BASSANIO:	Your answer to that.
SHYLOCK:	Antonio is a good man.
BASSANIO:	Have you heard any imputation to the contrary?
SHYLOCK:	Ho no, no, no, no. My meaning in saying he is a good man, is to have you understand me that he is sufficient – yet his means are in supposition: he hath an argosy bound to Tripolis, another to the Indies; I understand moreover upon the Rialto, he hath a third at Mexico, a fourth for England, and other ventures he hath squandered abroad. But ships are but boards, sailors but men; there be land-rats and water-rats, water-thieves and land-thieves, I mean pirates, and then there is the peril of waters, winds, and rocks. The man is notwithstanding sufficient. Three thousand ducats – I think I may take his bond.
BASSANIO:	Be assured you may.
SHYLOCK:	I will be assured I may. And that I may be assured, I will bethink me. May I speak with Antonio?
BASSANIO:	If it please you to dine with us.
SHYLOCK:	Yes, to smell pork, to eat of the habitation which your prophet the Nazarite conjured the devil into. I will buy with you, sell with you, talk with you, walk with you, and so following. But I will not eat with you, drink with you, nor pray with you. What news on the Rialto? What is he comes here?

Enter ANTONIO

BASSANIO:	This is Signior Antonio.
SHYLOCK:	[*Aside*] How like a fawning publican he looks. I hate him for he is a Christian. But more, for that in low simplicity He lends out money gratis, and brings down The rate of usance here with us in Venice. If I can catch him once upon the hip, I will feed fat the ancient grudge I bear him. He hates our sacred nation, and he rails Even there where merchants most do congregate, On me, my bargains, and my well-won thrift, Which he calls interest. Cursed by my tribe If I forgive him.

How does Shakespeare present Shylock here and elsewhere in the play?

---

5 Examine Shakespeare's presentation of Portia in the play *The Merchant of Venice*. How is she of central importance in the play?

She Stoops to Conquer – Goldsmith

1 Explore Goldsmith's presentation of Tony Lumpkin in *She Stoops to Conquer*. Do you think he develops during the course of the play?

2 How does Goldsmith create humour in *She Stoops to Conquer*?

3 Compare the presentation of the characters of Kate and Constance in *She Stoops to Conquer*.

4 How does Goldsmith make use of the contrast between town and country life in *She Stoops to Conquer*? What effect does this contrast create?

5 How does Marlow present an unusual 'hero figure' in *She Stoops to Conquer*?

The Importance of Being Earnest – Wilde

1 How is marriage presented in *The Importance of Being Earnest* and how do the characters respond to it?

2 How does Wilde make *The Importance of Being Earnest* funny?

You should write about:

- the dialogue
- characterisation
- humorous language
- any other ideas you find interesting.

3 Explore the presentation of one of the male/female relationships in *The Importance of Being Earnest*.

You should write about the relationship between:

- Algernon and Cecily, or
- Jack and Gwendolen, or
- Prism and Chasuble.

4 How does *The Importance of Being Earnest* present ideas to do with social class?

5 What issues does Wilde draw attention to in *The Importance of Being Earnest*?

QUESTION BANK ANSWERS

EXAMINER'S TIP

Remember that drama texts are written to be seen and heard rather than read. Always try to visualise the action as it might take place on the stage.

Much Ado About Nothing

❶ Here are some ideas.
  - Love is a major theme in the play.
  - The basic pattern can be seen as love begun; love challenged; love confirmed.
  - Look at the relationships between Claudio/Hero and Benedick/Beatrice.
  - Examine the other characters' views of love.

❷ Here are some ideas.
  - Don John rejects the advice of his servant, Conrade.
  - He is full of bitterness and resentment.
  - Don John's interest in the news that Claudio intends to marry Hero becomes the focus of his malice.
  - Views on Don John's influence on the play vary – you have to decide whether he is a stage villain, whether there are comic elements in his character, or whether he casts a dark shadow over the play.

❸ Here are some ideas.
  - Beatrice seems to imply that Benedick puts a stop to her comments.
  - She perhaps suggests that he does this because he cannot get the better of her in a verbal exchange.
  - 'I know you of old' suggests a long-standing association.
  - Their exchanges and love for each other provide both comedy and a contrast to other relationships in the play.

❹ Here are some ideas.
  - Claudio's images create a picture of the unwholesome and lustful.
  - He interprets all Hero's responses as affirmation of her guilt.
  - His language is suggestive of promiscuity.
  - You should form your own view of how Claudio is presented here.

❺ Here are some ideas.
  - Dogberry appears on the scene just at the point when Don John's plot is about to come to fruition.
  - Dogberry and Verges operate as a comic double act.
  - Their bumbling incompetence adds to the humour.

EXAMINER'S TIP

When thinking about characters, find as much evidence as you can, such as:
  - *what they look like*
  - *what they say and do*
  - *what they think (often we find out this through a character's soliloquies)*
  - *how they act*
  - *how they change as the play goes on*
  - *what others say about them.*

Romeo and Juliet

❶ Here are some ideas.
  - Romeo is devastated to hear of his banishment.
  - His passion overrides his reason.
  - His passionate and impulsive nature can be seen in various other parts of the play.
  - You should select two or three examples and explore them.

❷ Here are some ideas.
  - Mercutio adds wit and humour to the play through his wordplay.
  - His down-to-earth attitude towards love contrasts with Romeo's idealistic, emotional view of love.
  - The killing of Mercutio marks a turning point in the play and the whole tragedy stems from this incident.
  - Mercutio, being a relative of the Prince, involves the Prince directly in the feud.

❸ Here are some ideas.
  - The atmosphere is emotionally charged.
  - Both Paris and Romeo are grief stricken.
  - The darkness and the setting of the Capulet vault creates a dark and sombre atmosphere.
  - This heightens the sense of death and tragedy at the end of the play.

❹ Here are some ideas.
  - Both are young and fall in love at first sight.
  - They are both from important families.
  - Juliet is more cautious than Romeo.
  - Romeo acts much more on impulse.
  - Both show courage and are not afraid to die.
  - Both inspire pathos.
  - Both inspire love, loyalty and affection.

❺ Here are some ideas.
  - The tragedy hinges on fate.
  - You should explore some key examples, such as the accidental killing of Mercutio, the failure of Friar Lawrence's letter to reach Romeo, the friar's late arrival at the Capulet vault.

- There are references made to fate by both Romeo and Juliet.

EXAMINER'S TIP

Shakespeare often uses imagery to highlight and develop key ideas and themes.

The Merchant of Venice

❶ Here are some ideas.
- Money and money lending.
- Religion.
- Society and the outsider.
- Prejudice and stereotypes.
- Human relationships.
- You need to form your own judgements on the themes and examine how Shakespeare presents them.

❷ Here are some ideas.
- Antonio exhibits the love of a true friend to Bassanio.
- Bassanio and Portia triumph in love.
- They survive a quarrel, which shows their love is secure.
- Portia is successful in rescuing Antonio.

❸ Here are some ideas.
- Shylock voices a deeper religious divide.
- He expresses his outrage at the loss of Jessica to a Christian and his thirst for revenge.
- He recognises the Jews' and Christians' common humanity.

❹ Here are some ideas.
- His interest in making money is immediately apparent.
- He reveals his hatred for Christians and for Antonio in particular.
- He is a miser.
- The contrast (as presented by Shakespeare) between Christians and Jews is seen through him.
- The importance of religion is also apparent.
- He is shown to have ample reason for his hatred of Antonio.

❺ Here are some ideas.
- Portia expresses her feelings for being in a situation where she has no say in her choice of husband.
- She humorously runs through the list of her suitors' faults.
- She is beautiful, rich, intelligent and resourceful – all of which have important roles in the plot.
- Her key role is in the saving of Antonio.

She Stoops to Conquer

❶ Here are some ideas.
- Lumpkin is presented as a typical eighteenth- century country squire.

- At the beginning of the play, he is presented as a lazy wastrel.
- He shows his true colours and his ability to rise above petty squabbles when the elopement plot has been discovered.
- For much of the play he is a clever manipulator of the action.

❷ Here are some ideas.
- Much of the humour is derived from Goldsmith's use of dramatic irony.
- The main example of this is Marlow's delusion that he is staying at the inn.
- There are funny mistakes that occur, which the characters have to deal with.
- There are elements of caricature.
- There is a variety of quickly developing situations.

EXAMINER'S TIP

Make sure you are aware of the techniques that the dramatist uses in the play you are studying.

❸ Here are some ideas.
Kate
- She is presented as refined and very at ease in society.
- The first impression is of a dutiful daughter.
- We quickly learn she has manipulated the situation.
- She is also able to create a positive impression on Marlow.
- She is lively and imaginative.

Constance
- She has to take part in several pretences.
- She adopts a practical attitude towards her fortune.
- She shows constancy (as her name suggests).
- She provides a contrast to Kate.
- She is level-headed and faithful.

❹ Here are some ideas.
- Goldsmith gives the audience hints of London society seen through the eyes of Mrs Hardcastle and Marlow.
- He paints a picture of the moral neighbourhood through Hardcastle, Lumpkin and his rustic friends.
- Mrs Hardcastle does not want to conform to the stereotypical images of country living.
- The country girl conquering Marlow implies a triumph of the values of country over town.

❺ Here are some ideas.
- Marlow is a strange kind of hero.
- Most of the dramatic irony is at his expense.
- He is made a fool of by Lumpkin and Kate.

- He is laughed at by almost everyone.
- Goldsmith also has him displaying the sentiments that town audiences loved.

The Importance of Being Earnest

1 Here are some ideas.
- Marriage is called a number of things in the play.
- Many of the characters mock marriage.
- Even though so many characters frown on marriage, ironically, it is what all the action of the play moves towards.
- Algernon and Jack are motivated by their desire to marry.
- Marital troubles are presented.
- Lady Bracknell seems to have married for social prestige.
- The criticisms the play makes about marriage are a way of poking fun at society.

2 Here are some ideas.
- Much humour comes through the language.
- The plot presents a complex combination of events that build to an absurd climax.
- It pokes fun at social conventions and manners, vanities and hypocrisies.
- Humour comes from the ridiculous.
- The use of paradox.

3 Here are some ideas.
- Examine the language your chosen pair uses with each other.
- Each relationship has its own type of dialogue.
- Look at the social interactions of the characters.
- Look at how Wilde creates and fleshes out his characters.

4 Here are some ideas.
- Much of the play is social satire.
- Wilde makes fun of the absurdities and excesses in society.
- Much of the wit is targeted on what Wilde saw as the dry, stern and conservative nature of Victorian society.
- He saw these values embodied in the word 'earnest'.
- Hypocrisy of a society that pretends social class is important whereas it is really money that counts.

5 Here are some ideas.
Through the play, Wilde draws attention to a variety of issues:
- class
- money
- marriage
- beauty
- truth
- morality.

CHAPTER 6

Post-1914 drama

See also Chapter 8 in Letts *Revise GCSE English and English Literature*.

Try this sample GCSE question and then compare your answer with the Grade C and Grade A model answers on pages 79 to 81.

Spend about 40 minutes on this.

Leave enough time to read through and correct what you have written.

An Inspector Calls by J.B. Priestley

Just before he leaves, the Inspector tells the Birlings:

INSPECTOR: But just remember this. One Eva Smith has gone – but there are millions and millions and millions of Eva Smiths and John Smiths still left with us, with their lives, their hopes and fears, their suffering and chance of happiness, all intertwined with our lives, with what we think and say and do. We don't live alone. We are members of one body. We are responsible for each other. And I tell you that the time will soon come when, if men will not learn that lesson, then they will be taught it in fire and blood and anguish. Good night.

In the light of what the Inspector says here, examine the ways in which conflicting social attitudes are presented in the play.

These two answers are at grades C and A. Compare them with your answer and think about how you might have improved your own response.

GRADE C ANSWER

Kelly

Clear focus on the question and some relevant commentary.

We are introduced to the different lifestyles associated with social class at the very opening of the play 'An Inspector Calls'. ✓ We see the Birling family being waited on by Edna, a young parlourmaid. Social standing is an important aspect of the Birling family's existence. Mr Birling, a stereotypical factory owner, has got rich at the expense of the poor. In response to the Inspector when he asks him about him not paying more pay for his workers, Mr Birling says: '...if I'd agreed to this demand for a new rate we'd have added about twelve per cent to our labour costs.' ✓ It is clear that money and social standing is more important to Mr Birling than people are. When considering what impact Eva Smith's suicide has had, he states: 'But I care. I was almost certain for a knighthood in the next Honors list.'

Well-chosen supporting quotation.

Could be better expressed.

This being not bothered about others that is the main focus of the play and this is demonstrated through the treatment and suicide of Eva Smith. It appears that, just as everybody in the play have played some part in Evas death, Priestly, through the Inspector, 'inspects' us all. In the extract he takes the story of Eva and applies it to the whole of society: 'We don't live alone...We are responsible for each other' and, in this respect, we are all brought to account for our treatment of others.

This is a good point.

The difference in social class within the play is evident in a number of ways. For instance, we see a clear difference in social roles. On one hand, we see the workers in Birling's factory who are termed 'cheap labour' ✓ by the Inspector and the 'Women of the town' and on the other, the well-off lifestyle of the Birlings and those of equal social standing. The Inspector says 'Public men, Mr Birling, have responsibilities as well as priveleges.' however, the public men in the play seem to abuse their position rather than being of benefit to society as a whole. For example Alderman Meggarty, a 'respected citizen' is seen to be notorious for groping young girls, one girl going to visit him at the Town Hall 'managed to escape with a torn blouse'.

Good choice of quotation and use of example.

Good point here – some sense of staging.

Priestley also includes such elements in 'An Inspector Calls' to raise awareness of social class. ✓ For example, it is while the Birlings are drinking port and celebrating, that the young girl is admitted to hospital after drinking disinfectant which 'Burnt her insides out.' As the Inspector says, everyone 'helped to kill her' in some way, and that punishment will come to all involved 'If men will not learn that lesson, then they will be taught it in fire and blood and anguish'. ✓

Appropriate quotation to conclude essay.

SPELLCHECK!

privileges
benefit

14/25

> **Grade booster ⋯⟩ move C to B**
> - Greater development of ideas required.
> - More accurate expression needed.
> - Technical accuracy needs attention.

> These two answers are at grades C and A. Compare them with your answer and think about how you might have improved your own response.

GRADE A ANSWER

Good opening section.

Clear awareness of the structure and effect of the play and the relevance of the speech. Good support through well-chosen quotation.

Sound comment on characters and links to other parts of the play. A very well-made point.

Effectively developing the ideas and supporting them with well-chosen references to the text.

Manjit

This speech is the final speech made by the Inspector in 'An Inspector Calls' and in it he delivers his final message to the Birling family. ✓ This message is at the heart of the play and highlights the conflicting social attitudes presented in the play. The Inspector represents the view that we all live together in this world and that we all hold a social responsibility for each other. No one lives in a vacuum ✓ – as he says 'We are members of one body'. ✓

Throughout the play the Inspector has demonstrated this fact to them stage by stage showing how each member of the Birling family and Gerald Croft independently affected the life of Eva Smith and collectively drove her to her eventual suicide. ✓ These closing words draw together this message – that we all need to look after one another and treat each other in a caring and considerate way. Ominously, his final words contain a bleak warning:

> 'And I tell you that the time will soon come when, if men will not learn that lesson, then they will be taught it in fire and blood and anguish.'

The Inspector's words here seem to be especially aimed at Arthur and Sybil Birling. ✓ The views that they hold with regard to social attitudes and responsibility are completely the opposite ✓ to those expressed by the Inspector. Early on in the play Birling lectures the others about his views on social responsibility:

> '...a man has to make his own way – has to look after himself – and his family too, of course.' ✓

It is clear that he does not believe in looking after others and, in fact, sees those who do as 'cranks'. He goes on:

> '...the way some of these cranks talk and write now, you'd think everybody has to look after everybody else, as if we were all mixed up together like bees in a hive – community and all that nonsense.' ✓

The 'I'm alright Jack' attitude is then demonstrated when his dealings with Eva Smith are exposed he still accepts no responsibility ✓ even though it was he who sacked her in the first place simply for asking for a pay rise. He still holds the view that 'if you don't come down sharply on some of those people, they'd soon be asking for the earth.' As an employer he simply regards his workers as 'cheap labour'. ✓

Sybil Birling exhibits very similar attitudes towards those she sees as being beneath her. ✓ In fact both her and her husband are very concerned with their social position and the idea of keeping up appearances. At the end of the play, when they think the whole business had been a hoax they are just relieved that their behaviour will not be made public.

They have learnt nothing from the Inspector's visit and intend to carry on just as before and are surprised when Sheila and Eric do not see things like that. Birling complains: ✓

'They just won't try to understand our
position or to see the difference between
a lot of stuff like this coming out in
private and a downright public scandal.' ✓

The reason for this conflict of attitudes is that both Sheila and Eric have learnt something from the Inspector's visit. ✓ Both of them, at the start of the play, seem quite spoilt and shallow characters who only really think about themselves. However, as their involvement with Eva Smith and its consequences are revealed to them they at least begin to accept the responsibility of their own actions. ✓

22/25

Grade booster ····❯ move A to A*
- More detailed analysis needed of the attitudes shown by characters other than Birling.
- Needs more comment on the conflict of attitudes between the Birlings and Sheila and Eric.
- Should mention the attitude shown by Gerald Croft.

Spend about 45 minutes on each question in this section. Each question carries **25 marks**.

The Long and the Short and the Tall – Hall

1   Compare the ways in which the characters of Mitchem and Johnstone are presented in the play. How do you respond to these two characters?

2   Read the following extract carefully.

BAMFORTH:	…When the time comes, Smudge, it's going to be every man for himself.
EVANS:	Go on, man. Where could you make for?
BAMFORTH:	What's it matter? Anywhere but here. Desert Island. One that's loaded with bags of native bints wearing grass frocks. Settle down and turn native. Anything's better than ending up with Tojo's boys.
EVANS:	You'd never do it.
BAMFORTH:	That's all you know. Come down the beach and wave me off. If you've got time to wave with all them little Nippos on your trail. I'll be in the boat, Jack. Lying back and getting sunburnt with a basket of coconuts. (*'Cod' American.*) And so we say farewell to this lush, green and prosperous country of Malaya. As the sun sets in the west our tiny boat bobs peacefully towards the horizon. We take one last glimpse at the beautiful tropical coastline and can see, in the distance, our old comrade in arms and hopeless radio operator, Private Whitaker, making peace with the invading army of the Rising Sun – and the invading army of the Rising Sun is carving pieces out of Private Whitaker.
WHITAKER:	(*rising*) Pack it in, Bamforth.
BAMFORTH:	What's the matter, Whitto? Getting windy?
WHITAKER:	Just pack it in, that's all.
BAMFORTH:	Get knotted.
MACLEISH:	I haven't seen anybody handing medals to you yet, Bamforth.
BAMFORTH:	No, my old haggis basher. And you're not likely to. I've told you – I don't go a bundle on this death or glory stuff.
MACLEISH:	So why not keep your trap shut?
BAMFORTH:	Democracy, Mac. Free Speech. Votes for women and eight-double-seven Private Bamforth for Prime Minister.
SMITH:	Show us your Red Flag, Bammo.
BAMFORTH:	It's what we're fighting for. Loose living and six months' holiday a year. The General told me that himself. 'Bamforth,' he says to me, taking me round the back of the lav at Catterick. 'Bammo, my old son, the British Army's in a desperate position. The yellow peril's about to descend upon us, the gatling's jammed, the Colonel's dead and the cook corporal's stuffed the

> regimental mascot in the oven. On top of all that, and as if we
> hadn't got enough to worry about, we've got two thousand Jocks
> up the jungle suffering from screaming ab-dabs and going mad
> for women, beer and haggis. 'We're posting you out there,
> Bammo,' he says, 'to relieve the situation.' So before I had time
> to relieve myself, here I was.
>
> MACLEISH: And what have you got against the Jocks?
> BAMFORTH: Stroll on! He's off again! It's a joke, you thick-skulled nit!
> MACLEISH: And I'll not stand for any of your subordinations.
> BAMFORTH: Come on, boy! Come it on! Pull the tape on me again. That's
> all I want. I'll blanco your belt for you for twopence.
> MACLEISH: When you're on duty, Bamforth, you'll take orders like the rest.
> BAMFORTH: Get the ink dry in your pay-book first. You've not had the tape
> a month.
> MACLEISH: If I'm in charge here, that's all that matters, as far as you're
> concerned. It makes no difference to you if I've had the tape
> five minutes or five years. You'll jump to it, boy, when I'm
> calling out the time. You'll just do as you're told, or you're for
> the high jump. (BAMFORTH *swears under his breath and*
> *turns away.*)
> Bamforth! Bamforth, I'm talking to you!

How is Bamforth presented both here and elsewhere in the play?

3 What do you think the play has to say about the nature of war and the ways in which individuals respond to it?

4 Remind yourself of the part in Act 2 where Macleish and Mitchem hold a long conversation about the fate of the Japanese soldier. What do you learn about the character of Macleish from the conversation and from his actions elsewhere in the play?

5 Examine the function in the play of the following characters:

- Whitaker
- Evans
- Smith.

An Inspector Calls – Priestley

1 What is Mrs Birling's role in the play?

You should write about:

- her reactions to the Inspector
- her part in Eva Smith's fate
- her attitude to Eric and Sheila.

2 Read the following passage from Act 3 carefully.

BIRLING:	(*triumphantly*) There you are! Proof positive. The whole story's just a lot of moonshine. Nothing but an elaborate sell! (*He produces a huge sigh of relief.*) Nobody likes to be sold as badly as that – but – for all that – (*he smiles at them all*) Gerald, have a drink.
GERALD:	(*smiling*) Thanks, I think I could just do with one now.
BIRLING:	(*going to sideboard*) So could I.
MRS BIRLING:	(*smiling*) And I must say, Gerald, you've argued this very cleverly, and I'm most grateful.
GERALD:	(*going for his drink*) Well, you see, while I was out of the house I'd time to cool off and think things out a little.
BIRLING:	(*giving him a drink*) Yes, he didn't keep you on the run as he did the rest of us. I'll admit now he gave me a bit of a scare at the time. But I'd a special reason for not wanting any public scandal just now. (*Has his drink now, and raises his glass.*) Well, here's to us. Come on, Sheila, don't look like that. All over now.
SHEILA:	The worst part is. But you're forgetting one thing I still can't forget. Everything we said had happened really had happened. If it didn't end tragically, then that's lucky for us. But it might have done.
BIRLING:	(*jovially*) But the whole thing's different now. Come, come, you can see that, can't you? (*Imitating* INSPECTOR *in his final speech.*) You all helped to kill her. (*Pointing at* SHEILA *and* ERIC, *and laughing.*) And I wish you could have seen the look on your faces when he said that.
	SHEILA *moves toward door.*
	Going to bed, young woman?
SHEILA:	(*tensely*) I want to get out of this. If frightens me the way you talk.
BIRLING:	(*heartily*) Nonsense! You'll have a good laugh over it yet. Look, you'd better ask Gerald for that ring you gave back to him, hadn't you? Then you'll feel better.
SHEILA:	(*passionately*) You're pretending everything's just as it was before.
ERIC:	I'm not!
SHEILA:	No, but these others are.
BIRLING:	Well, isn't it? We've been had, that's all.
SHEILA:	So nothing really happened. So there's nothing to be sorry for, nothing to learn. We can all go on behaving just as we did.
MRS BIRLING:	Well, why shouldn't we?
SHEILA:	I tell you – whoever that Inspector was, it was anything but a joke. You knew it then. You began to learn something. And now you've stopped. You're ready to go on in the same old way.
BIRLING:	(*amused*) And you're not, eh?

ANSWERS ON PAGE 92 ANSWERS ON PAGE 92 ANSWERS ON PAGE 92 ANSWERS ON PAGE 92

SHEILA:	No, because I remember what he said, how he looked, and what he made me feel. Fire and blood and anguish. And it frightens me the way you talk, and I can't listen to any more of it.
ERIC:	And I agree with Sheila. It frightens me too.
BIRLING:	Well, go to bed then, and don't stand there being hysterical.
MRS BIRLING:	They're over-tired. In the morning they'll be as amused as we are.
GERALD:	Everything's all right now, Sheila. (*Holds up the ring.*) What about this ring?
SHEILA:	No, not yet. It's too soon. I must think.
BIRLING:	(*pointing to* ERIC *and* SHEILA) Now look at the pair of them – the famous younger generation who know it all. And they can't even take a joke–

What does the extract show about the ways in which the Inspector's visit has affected the characters?

How does this add to the dramatic impact of the ending of the play?

3 How does Priestly present Gerald in the play? Do you sympathise with him in any way as a character?

4 In Act 1 Birling tells Gerald and Eric:

BIRLING:	(*solemnly*) But this is the point. I don't want to lecture you two young fellows again. But what so many of you don't seem to understand now, when things are so much easier, is that a man has to make his own way – has to look after himself – and his family, too, of course, when he has one – and so long as he does that he won't come to much harm. But the way some of these cranks talk and write now, you'd think everybody has to look after everybody else, as if we were all mixed up together like bees in a hive – community and all that nonsense. But take my word for it, you youngsters – and I've learnt in the good hard school of experience – that man has to mind his own business and look after himself and his own...

How does this speech sum up Birling's attitude to life? How is his attitude important to events elsewhere in the play?

Death of a Salesman – Miller

 1 How does Miller present Biff Loman in the play? How does this character differ from both Willy and Happy?

2 Read the following passage carefully.

CHARLEY:	It's getting dark, Linda.
	LINDA *doesn't react. She stares at the grave.*
BIFF:	How about it, Mom? Better get some rest, heh? They'll be closing the gate soon.
	LINDA *makes no move. Pause.*
HAPPY	(*deeply angered*): He had no right to do that. There was no necessity for it. We would've helped him.
CHARLEY	(*grunting*): Hmmm.
BIFF:	Come along, Mom.
LINDA:	Why didn't anybody come?
CHARLEY:	It was a very nice funeral.
LINDA:	But where are all the people he knew? Maybe they blame him.
CHARLEY:	Naa. It's a rough world, Linda. They wouldn't blame him.
LINDA:	I can't understand it. At this time especially. First time in thirty-five years we were just about free and clear. He only needed a little salary. He was even finished with the dentist.
CHARLEY:	No man only needs a little salary.
LINDA:	I can't understand it.
BIFF:	There were a lot of nice days. When he'd come home from a trip; or on Sundays, making the stoop; finishing the cellar; putting on the new porch; when he built the extra bathroom; and put up the garage. You know something, Charley, there's more of him in that front stoop than in the sales he ever made.
CHARLEY:	Yeah. He was a happy man with a batch of cement.
LINDA:	He was so wonderful with his hands.
BIFF:	He had the wrong dreams. All, all, wrong.
HAPPY	(*almost ready to fight* BIFF): Don't say that!
BIFF:	He never knew who he was.
CHARLEY	(*stopping* HAPPY's *movement and reply. To* BIFF): Nobody dast blame this man. You don't understand; Willy was a salesman. And for a salesman, there is no rock bottom to the life. He don't put a bolt to a nut, he don't tell you the law or give you medicine. He's a man way out there in the blue, riding on a smile and a shoeshine. And when they start not smiling back – that's an earthquake. And then you get yourself a couple of spots on your hat, and you're finished. Nobody dast blame this man. A salesman is got to dream, boy. It comes with the territory.
BIFF:	Charley, the man didn't know who he was.
HAPPY	(*infuriated*): Don't say that!
BIFF:	Why don't you come with me, Happy?
HAPPY:	I'm not licked that easily. I'm staying right in this city, and I'm gonna beat this racket! (*He looks at* BIFF, *his chin set.*) The Loman Brothers!

BIFF:	I know who I am, kid.
HAPPY:	All right, boy. I'm gonna show you and everybody else that Willy Loman did not die in vain. He had a good dream. It's the only dream you can have – to come out number-one man. He fought it out here, and this is where I'm gonna win it for him.
BIFF	(*with a hopeless glance at* HAPPY, *bends toward his mother*): Let's go, Mom.
LINDA:	I'll be with you in a minute. Go on, Charley. (*He hesitates.*) I want to, just for a minute. I never had a chance to say good-bye.
	CHARLEY *moves away, followed by* HAPPY. BIFF *remains a slight distance up and left of* LINDA. *She sits there, summoning herself. The flute begins, not far away, playing behind her speech.*
LINDA:	Forgive me, dear. I can't cry. I don't know what it is but I can't cry. I don't understand it. Why did you ever do that? Help me, Willy, I can't cry. It seems to me that you're just on another trip. I keep expecting you. Willy, dear, I can't cry. Why did you do it? I search and search and I search, and I can't understand it, Willy. I made the last payment on the house today. Today, dear. And there'll be nobody home. (*A sob rises in her throat.*) We're free and clear. (*Sobbing more fully, released.*) We're free. (BIFF *comes slowly toward her.*) We're free...We're free...
	BIFF *lifts her to her feet and moves out up right with her in his arms.*
	LINDA *sobs quietly.* BERNARD *and* CHARLEY *come together and follow them, followed by* HAPPY. *Only the music of the flute is left on the darkening stage as over the house the hard towers of the apartment buildings rise into sharp focus.*

What is the importance of this final scene of the play?

3 What do you think are the main themes in *Death of a Salesman*? How does Miller present them?

4 What symbols or metaphors does Miller use in the play? What is their significance?

5 Remind yourself of the opening scene of the play where Willy and Linda are talking downstairs. How are Willy and Linda presented here? What ideas are introduced that are developed later in the play?

Hobson's Choice – Brighouse

1 Read the following passage carefully.

HOBSON:	Maggie, I'm just going out for a quarter of an hour.
MAGGIE:	Yes, father. Don't be late for dinner. There's liver.
HOBSON:	It's an hour off dinner-time (*Going*)
MAGGIE:	So that, if you stay more than an hour in the Moonraker's Inn you'll be late for it.
HOBSON:	'Moonraker's'? Who said – ? (*Turning*)
VICKEY:	If your dinner's ruined, it'll be your own fault.
HOBSON:	Well, I'll be eternally –
ALICE:	Don't swear, father.
HOBSON:	(*putting hat on counter*) No. I'll sit down instead. (He takes a chair, straddling across it and facing them with his elbows on its back.) Listen to me, you three. I've come to conclusions about you. And I won't have it. Do you hear that? Interfering with my goings out and comings in. The idea! I've a mind to take measures with the lot of you.
MAGGIE:	I expect Mr Heeler's waiting for you in 'Moonraker's', father.
HOBSON:	He can go on waiting. At present, I'm addressing a few remarks to the rebellious females of this house, and what I say will be listened to and heeded. I've noticed it coming on ever since your mother died. There's been a gradual increase of uppishness towards me.
VICKEY:	Father, you'd have more time to talk after we've closed tonight. (*She is anxious to resume her reading.*)
HOBSON:	I'm talking now, and you're listening. Providence has decreed that you should lack a mother's hand at the time when single girls grow bumptious and must have somebody to rule. But I'll tell you this, you'll none rule me.
VICKEY:	I'm sure I'm not bumptious, father.
HOBSON:	Yes, you are. You're pretty, but you're bumptious, and I hate bumptiousness like I hate a lawyer.
ALICE:	If we take trouble to feed you it's not bumptious to ask you not to be late for your food.
VICKEY:	Give and take, father.
HOBSON:	I give and you take, and it's going to end.
MAGGIE:	How much a week do you give us?
HOBSON:	That's neither here nor there. (Rises and moves to doors.) At the moment I'm on uppishness, and I'm warning you your conduct towards your parent's got to change. (*Turns to the counter.*) But that's not all. That's private conduct, and now I pass to broader aspects and I speak of public conduct. I've looked upon my household as they go about the streets, and I've been disgusted. The fair name and fame of Hobson have been outraged by members of Hobson's family, and uppishness has done it.
VICKEY:	I don't know what you're talking about.
HOBSON:	Vickey, you're pretty, but you can lie like a gasmeter. Who had new dresses on last week?
ALICE:	I suppose you mean Vickey and me?
HOBSON:	I do.
VICKEY:	We shall dress as we like, father, and you can save your breath.

HOBSON:	I'm not stopping in from my business appointment for the purpose of saving my breath.
VICKEY:	You like to see me in nice clothes.
HOBSON:	I do. I like to see my daughters nice. That's why I pay Mr Tudsbury, the draper, £10 a year a head to dress you proper. It pleases the eye and it's good for trade. But, I'll tell you, if some women could see themselves as men see them, they'd have a shock, and I'll have words with Tudsbury an' all, for letting you dress up like guys. I saw you and Alice out of the 'Moonraker's' parlour on Thursday night and my friend Sam Minns –
ALICE:	A publican.
HOBSON:	Aye, a publican. As honest a man as God Almighty ever set behind a bar, my ladies. My friend, Sam Minns, asked me who you were. And well he might. You were going down Chapel Street with a hump added to nature behind you.
VICKEY:	(*scandalized*) Father!
HOBSON:	The hump was wagging, and you put your feet on pavement as if you'd got chilblains – aye, stiff neck above and weak knees below. It's immodest!
ALICE:	It is not immodest, father. It's the fashion to wear bustles.
HOBSON:	Then to hell with the fashion.

How does Brighouse present the character of Hobson both here and elsewhere in the play?

2 At the end of the play, Maggie says to Willie: '*You're the man I've made you and I'm proud.*' How has Maggie '*made*' Willie and why do you think she is '*proud*'?

3 What do you think the play has to say about the accepted conventions between men and women?

Write about:

- attitudes to 'business'
- the relationship between Willie and Maggie
- Hobson's attitude towards Maggie, Alice and Victoria.

4 '*Courting's like that my love. All glitter and no use to anybody.*' Do you think this sums up Maggie's opinion of love and marriage?

5 Examine the function of TWO of the following characters in the play:

- Albert Prosser
- Fred Beenstock
- Mrs Hepworth
- Tubby Wadlow
- Jim Heeler
- Ada Figgins.

Pygmalion – Shaw

1   What is the importance of Colonel Pickering in *Pygmalion*?

Write about:

* his relationship with Higgins
* his attitude towards Eliza
* his role in the action of the play.

2   What does the character of Alfred Doolittle contribute to *Pygmalion*?

3   Read the following extract carefully.

HIGGINS:	[*in despairing wrath outside*] What the devil have I done with my slippers? [*He appears at the door*]
LIZA:	[*snatching up the slippers, and hurling them at him one after the other with all her force*] There are your slippers. And there. Take your slippers; and may you never have a day's luck with them!
HIGGINS:	[*astounded*] What on earth–! [*He comes to her*] Whats the matter? Get up. [*He pulls her up.*] Anything wrong?
LIZA:	[*breathless*] Nothing wrong – with you. Ive won your bet for you, havnt I? Thats enough for you. *I* dont matter, I suppose.
HIGGINS:	You won my bet! You! Presumptuous insect! *I* won it. What did you throw those slippers at me for?
LIZA:	Because I wanted to smash your face. I'd like to kill you, you selfish brute. Why didnt you leave me where you picked me out of – in the gutter? You thank God it's all over, and that now you can throw me back again there, do you? [*She crisps her fingers frantically*].
HIGGINS:	[*looking at her in cool wonder*] The creature is nervous, after all.
LIZA:	[*gives a suffocated scream of fury, and instinctively darts her nails at his face*]!!
HIGGINS:	[*catching her wrists*] Ah! would you? Claws in, you cat. How dare you shew your temper to me? Sit down and be quiet. [*He throws her roughly into the easy-chair*].
LIZA:	[*crushed by superior strength and weight*] Whats to become of me? Whats to become of me?
HIGGINS:	How the devil do I know whats to become of you? What does it matter what becomes of you?
LIZA:	You dont care. I know you dont care. You wouldnt care if I was dead. I'm nothing to you – not so much as them slippers.

HIGGINS:	[*thundering*] Those slippers.
LIZA:	[*with bitter submission*] Those slippers. I didnt think it made any difference now.
	A pause. ELIZA *hopeless and crushed. Higgins a little uneasy.*
HIGGINS:	[*in his loftiest manner*] Why have you begun going on like this? May I ask whether you complain of your treatment here?
LIZA:	No.
HIGGINS:	Has anybody behaved badly to you? Colonel Pickering? Mrs Pearce? Any of the servants?
LIZA:	No.
HIGGINS:	I presume you dont pretend that *I* have treated you badly.
LIZA:	No.
HIGGINS:	I am glad to hear it. [*He moderates his tone*]. Perhaps youre tired after the strain of the day. Will you have a glass of champagne? [*He moves towards the door*]
LIZA:	No. [*Recollecting her manners*] Thank you.
HIGGINS:	[*good-humoured again*] This has been coming on you for some days. I suppose it was natural for you to be anxious about the garden party. But thats all over now. [*He pats her kindly on the shoulder. She writhes*]. Theres nothing more to worry about.
LIZA:	No. Nothing more for you to worry about. [*She suddenly rises and gets away from him by going to the piano bench, where she sits and hides her face*]. Oh God! I wish I was dead.

How does Shaw present Higgins here and elsewhere in the play?

4   Remind yourself of the opening scene of the play. How effective do you find this scene as an opening to the play? How does it introduce the ideas and characters that will be developed later?

5   How does Shaw present Eliza in the play?

How do you respond to the ending of the play?

Post-1914 drama

EXAMINER'S TIP

Remember that drama texts are written to be seen and heard rather than read. Always try to visualise the action as it might take place on the stage.

The Long and the Short and the Tall

1. Here are some ideas.
   - Mitchem is the sergeant in charge of the patrol.
   - He has natural authority.
   - He quickly restores order when Macleish and Bamforth are about to fight.
   - He controls Bamforth with the use of sarcasm.
   - His attitude to war is cynical but realistic – he does his job regardless of what he thinks about it personally.
   - Johnstone is the corporal and is very different to Mitchem.
   - He lacks Mitchem's skill in handling people.
   - He tries to exert authority through brute force.
   - Unlike Mitchem his attitude towards the Japanese soldier is not governed by a practical approach to what is necessary but by a violent hatred of the enemy.
   - He is continuously cruel to the Japanese soldier.

2. Here are some ideas.
   - Bamforth is deeply cynical about the war.
   - He challenges authority and adopts a sarcastic attitude towards his superiors and fellow soldiers.
   - He shows a humane side when dealing with the Japanese prisoner.
   - In the end, Bamforth is the only one willing to defend the prisoner.

3. Here are some ideas.
   - The play is about war and attitudes to war.
   - Each of the characters shows a different attitude towards the war and towards the representation of the enemy – the Japanese soldier.
   - An examination of these different attitudes should be included.
   - The play does not present an anti-war stance but presents the moral dilemmas facing soldiers.

4. Here are some ideas.
   - Macleish has just been promoted to lance corporal and takes his role very seriously.
   - He is completely against killing the prisoner and refuses to accept Michem's view that it is necessary.
   - He feels he would rather give up his stripe than be involved in a cold-blooded killing.
   - In the end, though, he seems to accept that the life of the prisoner is not worth the lives of the patrol.

5. Here are some ideas.
   - Whitaker is a young, inexperienced soldier.
   - He is nervous and very jumpy.
   - Evans's relationship with Bamforth should be explored.
   - We learn about his girlfriend and his reading of his mother's women's magazine.
   - Smith's home life and wife and family images.
   - He tries to smooth tension.
   - Discuss what each of these characters adds to the play.

An Inspector Calls

1. Here are some ideas.
   - Mrs Birling represents a snobbish, socially superior attitude.
   - She supports the views held by Birling.
   - Her role in turning Eva Smith away from her committee, therefore bringing about the death of her own grandson, should be discussed.
   - She shows little understanding of her children, particularly Eric.

2. Here are some ideas.
   - The Inspector's visit has had more impact on Eric and Sheila.
   - They seem to have actually been changed by the realisation of what they have done.
   - Birling and Mrs Birling seem to want to continue as before when they think the whole thing has been a hoax.
   - The fact that they want to return to how things were before the Inspector's arrival and do not feel that they need to change their attitudes or behaviour in any way means the ending of the play has more impact on them – you should explain how this is so.

3. Here are some ideas.
   - Gerald has some of the characteristics of Birling and agrees with some of his ideas.
   - He is the son of a factory owner and agrees labour costs need to be kept down He believes Birling's behaviour regarding Eva Smith was completely reasonable.

- He does have a more humane side, though, and originally helps Eva, out of a sense of compassion. The Inspector comments that at least he made her happy for a time.
- At the end, however, he stands more with the Birlings than with Sheila and Eric.
- You will need to judge for yourself if you feel any sympathy for him as a character – remember to justify your views.

④ Here are some ideas.
- Birling's attitude is that a man should look after himself and his own and never mind anybody else.
- He has a selfish attitude, which he sees as a good, hard-headed businessman's approach to life.
- This attitude is exemplified in his dealings with Eva.
- His main concerns are making a profit and his public and social standing.

EXAMINER'S TIP

▶▶▶ *Make sure you are aware of the techniques that the dramatist uses in the play you are studying.*

Death of a Salesman
① Here are some ideas.
- Unlike Willy and Happy, Biff wants to find out the truth about himself.
- He acknowledges his failure and eventually confronts it.
- He wants to break through the lies surrounding his family in order to find the truth and come to terms with his own life.
- In the end, he breaks away from his father's dreams of him and his own dreams of himself.
- In the confrontation with his father, he shatters the Loman myth.

② Here are some ideas.
- This final scene shows Willy's funeral.
- Linda is surprised that no one attends the funeral except Charley, Willy's only friend.
- The scene shows the increasing gulf between Biff and Happy.
- Biff realises that Willy had the 'wrong dreams'.
- Happy defends Willy and shows that he intends to continue where his father left off.

③ Here are some ideas.
- The idea of reality versus illusion.
- The American Dream.
- Idealistic visions of success and happiness.
- Modern, capitalist driven society.

④ Here are some ideas.
- The jungle – 'the jungle is dark but full of diamonds' – Willy hopes to strike it rich.
- Diamonds represent tangible wealth.
- Stockings – represent both Willy's adultery and the falseness of Willy's existence.
- Seeds/garden – symbolise Willy's need for success.
- Tennis – Bernard's reference to tennis symbolises his success and the Lomans' failure.

⑤ Here are some ideas.
- The scene shows Willy's confusion.
- It reveals his troubled relationship with Biff.
- Linda appears apologetic for Biff and tries to smooth things over with Willy.
- Linda does not want to upset anyone but, later in the play, her conciliatory attitude does nothing to halt Willy's downward spiral.

EXAMINER'S TIP

▶▶▶ *Even a short extract can reveal a good deal about the characters and the ways in which the dramatist presents them.*

Hobson's Choice
① Here are some ideas.
- Hobson is a man with firm and definite ideas about how his daughters should behave.
- He is single-minded and likes his own way.
- He tries to live his life, run his house and dominate his daughters.
- He neglects his business and relies on his daughters' goodwill to run his shop and household.
- He is overbearing and self-important.
- The comedy comes from the mismatch between how he sees himself and how others see him.

② Here are some ideas.
- Maggie dominates and grooms Willie, who is seen as a weak character.
- She detects in Willie, though, some potential.
- She is determined and able to make him the man she wants to be proud of.
- Maggie brings out Willie's potential and transforms him from a humble bootmaker.

③ Here are some ideas.
- The conventional role of women in business as opposed to the role Maggie adopts.
- The dominance of Maggie in her relationship with Willie.
- Hobson attempts to exert male dominance over Maggie and her sisters.
- The relationships between men and women at the end of the play.

❹ Here are some ideas.
- Maggie is unconventional in her approach to 'courting'.
- She adopts a practical approach to marriage.
- She is business-like about it.
- You need to assess your own ideas with regard to whether you think this sums up her opinion of love and marriage.

❺ Here are some ideas.
- Albert Prosser and Fred Beenstock each play a part in Maggie's plotting against her father.
- Mrs Hepworth's function is to introduce us to Willie and later finance Willy and Maggie's business.
- Ada Figgins shows a contrast to Maggie and for the amusing scene of two women fighting over Willie.
- Jim Heeler is Hobson's confidant thus allowing us to hear his views.
- Tubby Wadlow is used to show the deterioration in Hobson's business.

EXAMINER'S TIP

> *Each character has a role to play in the drama and the dramatist presents them in such a way as to fulfil that role.*

Pygmalion

❶ Here are some ideas.
- Pickering presents a contrast to Higgins in a variety of ways.
- He is considerate towards Eliza.
- He represents the voice of reason and conventional attitudes and behaviour.
- This accentuates Higgins' eccentric behaviour.

❷ Here are some ideas.
- Doolittle adds colour and personality to the play.
- He makes no pretence to be virtuous but is completely honest about his nature.
- He presents his own philosophy centred on the idea of 'Undeserving Poor'.
- The higher he rises in the world, the less happy he becomes.

❸ Here are some ideas.
- Higgins is short-tempered and eccentric.
- He shows little sensitivity or understanding of Eliza.
- He also has a certain innocent quality.
- His own view of himself as an amiable, mild-mannered man is at odds with the way others see him.
- He likes to get his own way and will ride roughshod over everyone to achieve his ends.
- He is completely devoted to his work.

❹ Here are some ideas.
- Many of the major characters in the play are introduced in this opening scene.
- The device of the rainstorm is an effective one to draw people together.
- The character with the notebook intrigues the audience.
- Later, the idea of language and speech is introduced when it is revealed he has been noting down Eliza's speech in a phonetic alphabet.
- You will need to arrive at your own assessment of how effective you find this scene as an opening to the play.

❺ Here are some ideas.
- We first see Eliza as a young woman ready to stand up for her rights.
- She is very ignorant of the world and comedy is created through this – she has never seen a bath, for example.
- She does have standards of behaviour.
- Eliza emerges as an attractive woman with both spirit and potential.
- By the end of the play, Eliza has become a different person inside as well as out.
- She also comes to understand Higgins.
- You will need to assess your own response to the ending of the play.

Centre number
Candidate number
Surname and initials

Letts **Examining Group**

General Certificate of Secondary Education

English Literature

Time: 2 hours 15 minutes

(includes recommended reading time of 15 minutes)

Instructions to candidates

- Use black of blue ink or ball-point pen
- Answer **three** questions. Answer **one** question from each of the three Sections: A, B and C.
- There are two questions set on each text. Answer **only one** question on each of your chosen texts.
- You are allowed to use copies of the texts you have studied but these **must not** be annotated in any way.

For Examiner's use only

1			
2			
3			
4			
5			
6			
7			
8			
9			
10			
11			
12			
Total			

Letts

EDUCATIONAL

Section A – Drama

Answer **one** question from this section.

You should give evidence from the text to support any points you make in your answer.

Much Ado About Nothing – William Shakespeare

EITHER

Question 1

Although Claudio and Hero are the central characters of the 'main plot', it is Beatrice and Benedick who really catch our attention. Why do you think this is?

OR

Question 2

Read again Act 3 Scene iv. What do you think this scene adds to the play?

The Merchant of Venice – William Shakespeare

EITHER

Question 3

Explore Shakespeare's presentation of Portia in the play.

OR

Question 4

Remind yourself of the opening scene of the play. How effectively does this scene prepare us for later developments in the play?

Letts

The Importance of Being Earnest – Oscar Wilde

EITHER

Question 5

Examine Wilde's presentation of Lady Bracknell in the play.

OR

Question 6

Do you think the play is simply a light comedy or does it have a more serious message?

An Inspector Calls – J B Priestley

EITHER

Question 7

Compare and contrast the attitudes shown by Sheila and Eric with those shown by their parents.

OR

Question 8

Examine in detail the techniques that the Inspector uses in order to draw information from each character.

[turn over

Pygmalion – George Bernard Shaw

EITHER

Question 9

Remind yourself of the final part of the play from

'*Eliza [desperate]: Oh, you are a cruel tyrant*'

to the end of the play.

How different is Eliza at the end of the play from the flower girl at the beginning?

OR

Question 10

How important do you think Alfred Doolittle is to the play as a whole?

You should think about:
- his relationship with his daughter
- the way he speaks
- the ideas he has about the working class
- whether you think he has changed by the end of the play.

The Long and the Short and the Tall – Willis Hall

EITHER

Question 11

How is Bamforth presented and what is his importance in the play?

OR

Question 12

What role does the Japanese prisoner play in *The Long and the Short and the Tall*?

Section B – Poetry

Answer **one** question from this section.

You should give evidence from the text to support any points you make in your answer.

AQA Anthology – Specification A

EITHER

Question 1

a) Compare Whitman's use of imagery in *Patrolling Barnegat* with Armitage's use of imagery in *Homecoming*.

b) Compare these two poems with another poem from the Pre-1914 Poetry Bank and one poem by Carol Ann Duffy.

OR

Question 2

Compare how Blake presents the relationship between child and parent in *The Little Boy Lost and The Little Boy Found* with three other poems – one other Pre-1914 poem, one by Seamus Heaney and one by Gillian Clarke.

AQA Anthology – Specification B *Best Words* (Pre-1914)

EITHER

Question 3

Compare the effectiveness of Keats' description in *To Autumn* with another poem of your choice from the Pre-1914 selection in which the poet uses vivid description.

OR

Question 4

Compare the ways in which Browning tells a story in his poem Porphyria's Lover with another poem of your own choice from the selection in which the poets tells a story.

[turn over

The General Prologue – Geoffrey Chaucer

EITHER

Question 5

What impression do you form of life in Chaucer's time from the ways in which he presents his characters in the *General Prologue*? In your answer you should examine:

* the nature of the characters presented
* different kinds of emphases in the descriptions
* the contrasting aspects of Medieval society.

OR

Question 6

Choose two pilgrims from the *General Prologue* who are very different in nature and examine the ways in which Chaucer creates a vivid impression of them.

AQA Anthology Specification B – Best Words (Post-1914)

EITHER

Question 7

Explore the ways in which Plath uses imagery in *Mirror* and compare this with one other poem from the Post-1914 selection in which the poet uses vivid imagery.

OR

Question 8

Examine the ways in which Duffy explores her ideas in *War Photographer* and compare this poem with one other from the Post-1914 selection in which you have found the poet's ideas interesting.

War Poems – ed. Christopher Martin

EITHER

Question 9

Examine the ways in which Owen uses imagery to achieve his effects in his poems *Dulce Et Decorum Est* and *Disabled* and compare these poems with one other poem of your choice from the Post-1914 selection.

OR

Question 10

Choose two poems from the Post-1914 selection that express differing views of war. Explore the ways in which the poets express their ideas and achieve their effects.

Axed Between the Ears – ed. David Kitchen

EITHER

Question 11

Compare *Old Age Report* by Adrian Mitchell and *Beautiful Old Age* by D H Lawrence. You should comment in detail on the ways in which the poets use language to express their ideas.

OR

Question 12

Choose two poems from the selection that focus on the plight of animals and examine the ways in which the poets express their ideas.

[turn over

Section C – Prose

Answer one question from this section.

You should give evidence from the text to support any points you make in your answer.

Hard Times – Charles Dickens

EITHER

Question 1

The following description of Mr Gradgrind is taken from the beginning of the novel.

> 'Now, what I want is, Facts. Teach these boys and girls nothing but Facts. Facts alone are wanted in life. Plant nothing else, and root out everything else. You can only form the minds of reasoning animals upon Facts: nothing else will ever be of any service to them. This is the principle on which I bring up these children. Stick to Facts, sir!'
>
> 'The scene was a plain, bare, monotonous vault of a schoolroom, and the speaker's square forefinger emphasised his observations by underscoring every sentence with a line on the schoolmaster's sleeve. The emphasis was helped by the speaker's square wall of a forehead, which had his eyebrows for its base, while his eyes found commodious cellarage in two dark caves, overshadowed by the wall. The emphasis was helped by the speaker's mouth, which was wide, thin, and hard set. The emphasis was helped by the speaker's voice, which was inflexible, dry, and dictatorial. The emphasis was helped by the speaker's hair, which bristled on the skirts of his bald head, a plantation of firs to keep the wind from its shining surface, all covered with knobs, like the crust of a plum pie, as if the head had scarcely warehouse-room for the hard facts stored inside. The speaker's obstinate carriage, square coat, square legs, square shoulders – nay, his very neckcloth, trained to take him by the throat with an unaccommodating grasp, like a stubborn fact, as it was – all helped the emphasis.
>
> 'In this life, we want nothing but Facts, sir; nothing but Facts!'
>
> The speaker, and the schoolmaster, and the third grown person present, all backed a little, and swept with their eyes the inclined plane of little vessels then and there arranged in order, ready to have imperial gallons of facts poured into them until they were full to the brim.

How does Dickens present Gradgrind both here and elsewhere in the novel?

OR

Question 2

How does Dickens present his characters and make them stand out as individuals? You should write about **three** characters to illustrate your answer.

Letts

Leave blank

EITHER

Question 3

In Chapter IX, Catherine tells Nelly:

'It would degrade me to marry Heathcliff now; so he shall never know how I love him: and that, not because he's handsome, Nelly, but because he's more myself than I am. Whatever our souls are made of, his and mine are the same; and Linton's is as different as a moonbeam from lightning, or frost from fire.'

What is the importance of this speech? How does Bronte present Cathy's love for Heathcliff?

OR

Question 4

Examine the key themes in *Wuthering Heights* and the ways in which Bronte explores them.

[turn over

Letts

Leave blank

EITHER

Question 5

This passage describes Boldwood's response to the letter sent anonymously by Bathsheba on St. Valentine's Day.

> When Boldwood went to bed he placed the valentine in the corner of the looking-glass. He was conscious of its presence, even when his back was turned upon it. It was the first time in Boldwood's life that such an event had occurred. The same fascination that caused him to think it an act which had a deliberate motive prevented him from regarding it as an impertinence. He looked again at the direction. The mysterious influences of night invested the writing with the presence of the unknown writer. Somebody's – some *woman's* – hand had travelled softly over the paper bearing his name; her unrevealed eyes had watched every curve as she formed it; her brain had seen him in imagination the while. Why should she have imagined him? Her mouth – were the lips red or pale, plump or creased? - had curved itself to a certain expression as the pen went on – the corners had moved with all their natural tremulousness: what had been the expression?
>
> The vision of the woman writing, as a supplement to the words written, had no individuality. She was a misty shape, and well she might be, considering that her original was at that moment sound asleep and oblivious of all love and letter-writing under the sky. Whenever Boldwood dozed she took a form, and comparatively ceased to be a vision: when he awoke there was the letter justifying the dream.

What do his reactions here tell you about his character? What is the importance of this incident to what happens later in the novel?

OR

Question 6

Explore Hardy's presentation of Gabriel Oak.

To Kill a Mockingbird – Harper Lee

EITHER

Question 7

Remind yourself of the passage in Chapter 10 where Atticus breaks down the Ewells' story that Tom Robinson raped Mayella. What is the importance of this incident in the novel as a whole?

Write about:

- what you learn about the Ewells from this section
- what you learn about the attitudes of the characters
- ideas in this section that are important in the novel as a whole.

OR

Question 8

How does *To Kill a Mockingbird* examine the theme of justice?

EITHER

Question 9

The following passage is taken from the end of Chapter Eight.

'You are a silly little boy,' said the Lord of the Flies, 'just an ignorant, silly little boy.'

Simon moved his swollen tongue but said nothing.

'Don't you agree?' said the Lord of the Flies. 'Aren't you just a silly little boy?'

Simon answered him in the same silent voice.

'Well then,' said the Lord of the Flies, 'you'd better run off and play with the others. They think you're batty. You don't want Ralph to think you're batty, do you? You like Ralph a lot, don't you? And Piggy, and Jack?'

Simon's head was tilted slightly up. His eyes could not break away and the Lord of the Flies hung in space before him.

'What are you doing out here all alone? Aren't you afraid of me?'

Simon shook.

'There isn't anyone to help you. Only me. And I'm the Beast.'

Simon's mouth laboured, brought forth audible words.

'Pig's head on a stick.'

'Fancy thinking the Beast was something you could hunt and kill!' said the head. For a moment or two the forest and all the other dimly appreciated places echoed with the parody of laughter. 'You knew, didn't you? I'm part of you? Close, close, close! I'm the reason why it's no go? Why things are what they are?'

The laughter shivered again.

'Come now,' said the Lord of the Flies. 'Get back to the others and we'll forget the whole thing.'

Simon's head wobbled. His eyes were half-closed as though he were imitating the obscene thing on the stick. He knew that one of his times was coming on. The Lord of the Flies was expanding like a balloon.

'This is ridiculous. You know perfectly well you'll only meet me down there— so don't try to escape!'

Simon's body was arched and stiff. The Lord of the Flies spoke in the voice of a schoolmaster.

'This has gone quite far enough. My poor, misguided child, do you think you know better than I do?'

There was a pause.

'I'm warning you. I'm going to get waxy. D'you see? You're not wanted. Understand? We are going to have fun on this island. Understand? We are going to have fun on this island! So don't try it on, my poor misguided boy, or else—'

Simon found he was looking into a vast mouth. There was blackness within, a blackness that spread.

'—Or else,' said the Lord of the Flies, 'we shall do you. See? Jack and Roger and Maurice and Robert and Bill and Piggy and Ralph. Do you. See?'

Simon was inside the mouth. He fell down and lost consciousness.

How does Golding present Simon's 'meeting'? How is Simon an important character in *Lord of the Flies*?

OR

Question 10

What, in your view, are the central themes of *The Lord of the Flies*? How does Golding explore them throughout the novel?

Of Mice and Men – John Steinbeck

EITHER

Question 11

Choose two scenes from the story that you have found effective and examine closely Steinbeck's style of writing in each of these scenes, saying why you find each of them particularly striking.

OR

Question 12

Which two characters do you feel most sympathy for in the novel and why?

Answers to mock examination papers

The points that you are given on each question in this section are suggestions of the kinds of things you could write about in an answer. Remember that literature questions do not have 'right' or 'wrong' answers and each of the questions could be answered in a variety of ways.

Section A – Drama

Question 1

- The wit of Beatrice and her strength of character.
- The wordplay between her and Benedick.
- The 'colourful' nature of both characters.
- The development of their love as the play goes on.

Question 2

- Hero prepares for her wedding.
- Her mood seems to be a portent of the coming disaster.
- Margaret's earthy wit creates a contrast to Hero's mood.
- The dramatic irony adds a sense of tension.
- Tension is maintained through the superficial lightness of the scene and the audience's awareness of what is to come.

Question 3

- She is a dutiful daughter obeying the wishes of her dead father.
- She appears passive.
- Her comments on her suitors show her shrewd mind.
- She is selfless in her response to Antonio's plight.
- She sheds her passive role and saves Antonio.

Question 4

- The play opens with Antonio feeling very melancholy.
- There is discussion of the ships in which he has invested all his wealth.
- Antonio speaks to Bassanio about his plans to woo a lady.

- Bassanio has no money so Antonio borrows it to lend him.
- These elements form the basis of the plot.

Question 5

- Discuss Lady Bracknell's role in the play.
- Examine her relationships with other characters.
- Look at the values she holds.

Question 6

- You need to work out your own ideas and feelings about the play here.
- It would be worth thinking about any social criticism of Victorian society Wilde makes.
- Think about the little foibles and idiosyncrasies of human behaviour he focuses on.

Question 7

- Sheila and Eric are affected by the Inspector's visit.
- Their consciences are touched by their roles in Eva's death.
- Their attitudes and behaviour change.
- Birling and his wife are untouched.
- They think about their own positions.
- They do not change.

Question 8

- The Inspector's use of photographs.
- His use of 'shock' tactics, such as telling Mrs Birling she had seen Eva Smith only a few days before.
- His presentation of 'factual' information.
- How he gets the characters to tell their own stories.

Question 9

- Eliza has changed the ways she speaks.
- She has found independence.
- She has developed as a character.
- Her relationships with her father and Higgins have changed.

Question 10

- Explore Doolittle's relationship with Eliza.
- Think about the way he speaks.
- Look at his philosophy regarding the 'undeserving poor'.
- Look at his attitude towards his changed fortune.

Question 11

- Discuss Bamforth's rebellious attitude.
- Think about the contrast he provides with other characters.
- Look at his attitude towards the Japanese prisoner.

Question 12

- The Japanese prisoner represents 'the enemy'.
- He brings out different kinds of behaviour among the other characters.
- He allows other characters to talk about moral questions in relation to war.
- He is a reminder of the threat facing them.

Section B – Poetry

Question 1

a)
- Pick out specific images and describe the effects they create.
- Make sure you compare the techniques of the two poets.

b)
- Select the poems that you compare with the first two, carefully ensuring that you have plenty to write about.
- Make sure you select them from the Pre-1914 Poetry Bank.

Question 2

- The central focus of your answer should be on relationships so select your poems for comparison accordingly.
- Make sure you follow the instructions of the question carefully.

Question 3

- Begin by focusing on *To Autumn*.
- Your analysis of Keats' descriptive technique should centre on his use of imagery in this poem.
- Choose the poem you are going to compare with *To Autumn* carefully, making sure it is one in which the poet uses vivid description.

Question 4

- Your focus should be on the ways in which the poets tell stories.
- Make sure your poem for comparison is one that tells a story of some kind.

- Write about specific techniques that the poets use, commenting on features of language.

Question 5

- Focus on the context of the tale.
- Do not try to write about all the characters – select ones to illustrate specific points.
- Examine the ways in which Chaucer presents his characters within the context of Medieval society.

Question 6

- This question gives you a free choice of the characters you choose to write about.
- Select your characters carefully, making sure they are very different.
- Examine how Chaucer gives a vivid impression of them – this will involve looking carefully at the details of the language he uses to describe them.

Question 7

- The main focus of this question is on *Mirror* and on the ways in which Plath uses imagery.
- Make sure you analyse the effects of the imagery, using specific details from the text to illustrate your comments.
- Select the poem you are using for comparison carefully, making sure it is one in which the poet uses imagery.

Question 8

- The focus of this question is *War Photographer* and you need to examine carefully how Duffy explores her ideas.
- Select your comparison poem carefully, making sure it is one that you have ideas about.
- Remember that you need to analyse specific details of the ways in which the poets use language.

Question 9

- Vivid description and use of imagery is likely to be at the centre of your response to *Dulce Et Decorum Est* and, in a different way, in *Disabled* too.
- Select the other poem for comparison carefully, making sure you have plenty of ideas about it.

Question 10

- This question gives you a free choice in the poems you write about.
- Select your poems carefully, making sure you have plenty to say about them.
- Remember that the main focus of your answer should be on the ways the poets express their ideas and achieve their effects.

- This means you need to write about the language the poets use, picking out specific details and analysing the effects they create.

Question 11

- Make sure your response has a comparative structure – don't simply write about one poem and then write about the other.
- Make sure you examine in detail the ways in which the poets use language.
- Use quotations to support your ideas.

Question 12

- This question gives you a free choice in the poems you write about.
- Select your poems carefully, making sure the focus is on the plight of animals and ensuring you have plenty to say about them.
- Remember that the main focus of your answer should be on the ways the poets express their ideas and achieve their effects.
- This means you need to write about the language the poets use, picking out specific details and analysing the effects they create.

Section C – Prose

Question 1

- Gradgrind is a man who places total importance on facts.
- He believes completely in his philosophy.
- He uses his own children as part of his educational experiment.
- He does show that he can change and learn from his experiences.

Question 2

- The names he gives them are in keeping with their characters, for example M'Choakumchild.
- He identifies them with specific roles in society.
- He often uses rich figurative language to describe them.
- He exaggerates characteristics and uses a form of caricature.
- Select your examples well to illustrate your points.

Question 3

- Catherine's acceptance of Edgar's proposal marks the turning point in the plot.
- Heathcliff leaves after he has overheard Catherine's words here.

- Her love for Heathcliff is presented in images of them being as one person.
- They both possess a 'wild' nature and Cathy says 'I am Heathcliff'.
- Ultimately, this love is shown to be a powerful but destructive force.

Question 4

- The destructiveness of love is explored through the relationship of Cathy and Heathcliff.
- The second love story ends happily and peace is restored to Wuthering Heights.
- Social class is explored through the Earnshaws and Lintons.
- The conflict between Nature and Culture – Nature is represented by the Earnshaw family and Culture by the Lintons.

Question 5

- On the surface, Boldwood seems reserved and remote but, when he receives the valentine from Bathsheba, strong emotions are revealed.
- The passage shows the extent of the effect that the valentine has had on him as he imagines in his mind's eye the woman who sent it and even dreams of her when he sleeps.
- The valentine changes his whole life and the locals are amazed when he organises a party.
- His love for Bathsheba is expressed by him wanting to possess her.
- He tries to make her happy but is driven by a passion that is destructive.
- In the end, the culmination of this passion is his murder of Troy.

Question 6

- Gabriel Oak is a strong character who persists even when things go wrong for him.
- He is a good farmer and is both unsentimental and caring towards his animals.
- He has a quiet dignity.
- As a lover he is less successful, but he offers Bathsheba an unselfish and sincere love.
- He is patient and has much personal integrity.
- He contrasts with the other major characters in that he has truth and honesty to him and he sticks to his principles throughout.

Question 7

- The Ewells are poor.
- They show great prejudice against the black people.
- Bob Ewell makes up for his own lack of importance by taking it out on others.
- He has no sense of justice or fairness.
- In the novel they highlight the theme of prejudice.

Question 8

- Atticus believes firmly in justice.
- He does all he can to see that justice is done at the trial of Tom Robinson.
- Even so, it is clear that there is no justice for the black people.
- This is illustrated in what happens to Tom Robinson.
- There is no justice in the social hierarchy.

Question 9

- Simon is an outsider to the group.
- He represents a spiritual aspect – his experience is almost vision-like.
- He is a loner when all the other boys seek to be part of a group.
- He is the one who discovers the true nature of the 'beast'.
- His 'conversation' with The Lord of the Flies is a prophetic warning.
- His killing unleashes the brutal, tribal nature of the boys as he is ritualistically killed.

Question 10

- The way in which 'civilised' society is fragile and can soon break down.
- Primitive human instincts lie just below the surface.
- The need for social grouping.
- The struggle for power.
- Good versus evil.
- The dominance of the strong over the weak.

Question 11

- You have a free choice of passage in this question. Make sure you select passages that you can write about.
- Focus on the specific details of how Steinbeck uses language and the effects created.

Question 12

- You are free to choose whichever characters you want to answer this question.
- The main thing is to be able to explain why you feel sympathetic towards them.
- This should relate to how Steinbeck presents them – again a focus on the language.

Index

The publisher and authors would like to thank the following for permission to use copyright material. Every effort has been made to contact copyright holders of material reproduced in this book. Any omissions will be rectified in subsequent printings if notice is given to the publisher.

Extracts from *Of Mice and Men* by John Steinbeck (Penguin, 2000) ©John Steinbeck, 1937, 1965; Extracts from *Lord of the Flies* by William Golding, ©William Golding, used by permission of Faber and Faber Limited; *I'm the King of the Castle*, ©Susan Hill, 1970, used by permission of Sheil Land Associates Ltd; *A Kestrel for a Knave* by Barry Hines (Michael Joseph, 1968) ©Barry Hines, 1968, used by permission of Penguin Books Ltd; *To Kill a Mockingbird*, by Harper Lee, published by Heinemann. Used by permission of The Random House Group Limited; Extract reproduced from *An Inspector Calls* by J. B. Priestley (Copyright ©J. B. Priestley 1947) by permission of PFD on behalf of the Estate of J. B. Priestley; Extract from *The Long and The Short and The Tall*, reproduced by permission of The Agency (London) Ltd, ©Willis Hall, First published by Heinemann, all rights reserved and enquiries to The Agency (London) Ltd, 24 Pottery Lane, London W11 4LZ info@theagency.co.uk; Extract from *Death of a Salesman*, by Arthur Miller, ©1949 by Arthur Miller, reprinted by permission of International Creative Management, Inc.; Extract from *Hobson's Choice* by Harold Brighouse reprinted by permission of the publishers, Samuel French Ltd, on behalf of the Estate of Harold Brighouse; Extract from *Pygmalion* by Bernard Shaw, used by permission of The Society of Authors, on behalf of the Bernard Shaw Estate.